SONGS
for
SUFFERING

Hannah,

May this book be
a great blessing to you

Lots of love,

Dad

SONGS
for
SUFFERING

Praying the Psalms
in Times of Trouble

SIMON P. STOCKS

Songs for Suffering: Praying the Psalms in Times of Trouble

© 2017 Hendrickson Publishers Marketing, LLC
P. O. Box 3473
Peabody, Massachusetts 01961-3473
www.hendrickson.com

ISBN 978-1-61970-880-8

The quotation of Artur Weiser on page 61 is taken from *The Psalms: A Commentary* (Philadelphia: Westminster, 2000), 819.

Printed in the United States of America

First Printing—March 2017

Library of Congress Cataloging-in-Publication Data

A catalog record for this title is available
from the Library of Congress
Hendrickson Publishers Marketing, LLC ISBN 978-1-61970-841-9

Acknowledgements

This book could not have been produced without the support and input of the following people, to whom I record here my gratitude:

Philip Jenson, Coulsdon Churches Lent Study Group, Philip Duce, Kate Byrom, Karen Stocks, the New Wine Network Croydon Core Group, Sarah Manouch, the guy in the Fedex office, Gwen Knight and companions, colleagues at St. Augustine's College of Theology, and Carl Nellis and the team at Hendrickson.

OVERVIEW OF CONTENTS

"WHAT'S COMING UP . . . ?"

"O MY GOD!"

There are times when I have felt unable to pray because of the pain or turmoil that I was going through. Bereavement, family breakdown, prolonged illness, betrayal by a friend . . . I'm not alone in any of these. This is the normal stuff of life.

So I have written this book for anyone who is going through tough times, whatever form that takes. The book is intended simply to help you to pray. It is a book about finding a way through, when there does not appear to be one.

By "praying" I do not only mean "asking God for help," though that surely is very significant in times of distress. But I have in mind the whole spectrum of ways of talking to God, whatever form that takes.

Perhaps you are praying already. Even the cry of "O my God!" can be a prayer, if it is meant that way. It's not a bad starting point. I want to help you to build on it and add to it, in a way that has real resonance with your situation.

Perhaps you are not praying yet. If that's the case, I want to encourage you to find your voice and express yourself to God. After all, that's prayer. No matter how you feel, you matter and your voice matters.

Most of the examples I will give will come from the book of Psalms, the prayer book of the Bible. This wonderful book has been passed down through the centuries by so many people of faith. It offers us the tried and tested means to pray in just about any situation imaginable. It offers us soaring hymns of praise, confessions, heartfelt pleas, and songs of thanksgiving. Most importantly for those who are suffering, it includes many prayers that express the full measure of human pain and need. These are known as psalms of lament.

The psalms have tremendously enriched my own prayers, and so I offer to you the wonderful ways in which they have helped me. Having said that, the language of the psalms can be alien to us, and I still find it difficult at times. Please don't be put off by that. The psalms can still offer us a model and a pattern of prayer, even if we don't use their exact words.

The psalms of lament tend to express the most extreme cases of suffering, which is what makes them usable in any situation, whether extreme or not. I have written this book in the same way, generally with the most serious situations in mind. It is intended, therefore, to be of use in any difficulty. Don't think "Well, my situation isn't that bad." Every situation is bad enough for the people concerned, and the principles explained in this book will be relevant.

So I offer you the psalms and the ideas explored in this book so that you can make them your own. May you find deeper connection to God as you do so, even in the toughest of times.

CHAPTER 1

"I FEEL AWFUL."

Down in the Dumps

There are times when we feel awful: bad, down, fed up, depressed, frustrated, despairing, wound up, hopeless. Call it what you will. Sometimes words fail—we can't even begin to express how we feel. Or perhaps we can, but not in a form of words we would want anyone else to hear. Difficult, negative feelings can be very real and very strong. Sometimes I feel them eating me away from inside and threatening to extend outward, gradually tainting more and more of my life with their malignant presence. At other times they seem to be "out there," hemming us in, holding us down, engulfing us and thwarting any attempt to avoid them.

So this is where we begin: in the reality of strong negative feelings, feelings that at least some of the time seem to have the upper hand over us. We are in the place that the psalmist refers to as "the depths." Quite what this means is up to our imagination. It is a low place, very far down. To me it suggests darkness and loneliness, cut off from the light and life of those people and places we love. It suggests a sense of great loss, as we might say "brought low," or perhaps "put down." In the Bible it usually refers to deep water or the sea. In the psalms (69:2, 14; 130:1) it is a figurative description and implies being engulfed, in a place of great danger and threat to the psalmist's well-being and security. In Isaiah 51:10 and Ezekiel 27:34 it refers literally to the depths of the sea, and this also has connotations of primitive chaos and evil, symbolizing everything that is contrary to God's goodness in the created order of things.

Can't Get round It

When Isaiah refers to the depths, he is doing so in a situation of distress, remembering how God had done great things in the past and longing for the same help again.

> Awake, awake, put on strength,
>   O arm of the LORD!
> Awake, as in days of old,
>   the generations of long ago!
> Was it not you who cut Rahab in pieces,
>   who pierced the dragon?
> Was it not you who dried up the sea,
>   the waters of the great deep;
> who made the depths of the sea a way
>   for the redeemed to cross over?
>   (Isaiah 51:9–10)

The idea of God making a road through the depths of the sea so people might cross over is a reference to the great story of the exodus, of God saving people who were in very great distress, their lives under threat. Isaiah spoke on behalf of a people who were equally distraught and ached for God to lead them through their time of trouble.

Like the depths of the sea that faced the ancient Israelites, the depths that we face cannot be avoided. There's no way round. What we need is to find a way through them, so that we are not overwhelmed. We might dare to believe that God can make a road through for us, or we might feel that God is asleep or absent or simply inattentive to our situation. But to find a way through is what we need.

How do we do that? What can we do when we are in "the depths," when we are feeling "out of our depth," and we feel engulfed, threatened, or overwhelmed? We might have received some terrible news or suffered a tragic loss. We might be in a relationship that seems broken beyond repair. We might be struggling with feelings of intense rage or jealousy or bitterness that seem beyond our control. We may be fearful for our security for the future. We might feel betrayed. We might have lost a sense of purpose, so that everything seems pointless. What can we do?

I Don't Want to Talk about It

One of the worst aspects of such a situation is if it cuts us off from other people. Communication is hard. I've known people who, when times are tough, stop going to church because they can't face other people. I know myself that it feels like rubbing salt into the wound when someone asks "How are you?" assuming the answer will be "Alright." What do you say instead? "Mustn't grumble"? "Could be worse"? Giving an honest answer is sometimes too embarrassing to contemplate, and the idea of avoiding painful feelings by not talking about them is a popular one. Back in 1977, Rod Stewart topped the UK singles chart singing "I don't want to talk about it / how you broke my heart." In 1996 the most played song on American radio was No Doubt's "Don't speak . . . don't tell me 'cause it hurts." And more recently Snow Patrol had success on both sides of the Atlantic with "Chasing Cars," whose lyrics seem to me to describe a wished-for escape from reality and include "I don't quite know / how to say / how I feel."

But putting on a brave face and not talking about how we feel doesn't necessarily do our self-esteem any good. It means that we are ignoring the things that matter most to us at that moment. And by ignoring what matters most to us, it is almost as if we are ignoring ourselves, belittling our true self and replacing it with a cardboard cutout that always bears the same expression, no matter what.

Yet the reasons for not expressing our feelings honestly may be quite clear and quite strong. If we are honest, we open ourselves up to whatever response the other person might make, and that's not necessarily going to be helpful. Indeed, they might misunderstand or disrespect the nature of the situation we find ourselves in. And the more we have already endured other people's inappropriate responses, the less inclined we are to continue to take that chance. I remember a social occasion where the first three times I was asked "How are you?" I replied "Feeling terrible at the moment." Each time the other person made light of my response or just ignored it. After that I gave up and just said I was "Fine." Perhaps I shouldn't have gone out that night at all!

Besides having to cope with other people's reactions, we may be thinking that it's wrong to feel the way we do, or at least wrong to express such feelings. This can particularly be the case in a church context where there is an emphasis on celebration and rejoicing in God's love and the hope of eternal life in Jesus. How on earth can my self-absorbed, painful, and messed-up thoughts find a place in that context?

These problems with communication are tragically ironic, given how important it is to find support and help from each other when we are in need. But in order to open ourselves up to the support and comfort of other people, we need to make ourselves vulnerable to them by being honest about how we feel. And the problem is that we feel we don't have the strength to be open and make ourselves vulnerable, because the response we get might be hurtful rather than helpful. And so we end up isolated in our turmoil, sinking ever deeper.

These problems are compounded when it comes to prayer. Not only might we feel personally too fragile to engage with how we really feel before God, there can also be a host of ideas and attitudes that get in the way. Is it wrong to feel the way we do? Oughtn't we to praise God at all times and in all places? Isn't it a sin to be angry or doubtful or self-pitying? Indeed, isn't our suffering an indication of our sinfulness for which God rightly chastises us? In which case, what right have we to express our discomfort to God? Or perhaps this time of trial is sent by God for our good, as part of the process of being made perfect in Christ? Or sharing in Christ's sufferings? So many reasons can crowd around our troubled minds for not praying to God out of the reality of our distress.

Hear My Voice!

In such a situation, what does the psalmist do?

Out of the depths I cry to you, O Lord.
   Lord, hear my voice! (Psalm 130:1–2a)

The psalmist cries! Cries aloud to God and expects to be heard. There is no holding back here. The Hebrew word used for "cry" implies a loud calling upon God. This is a full-blooded cry for help, not a polite request. And this is a wonderful example for us. The psalms have been the bedrock of Christian prayer for two thousand years, and they are ours still, to use today. So there's a great encouragement here for us to use the psalms as our own prayers, and not to hold back from telling God how it really is for us. The first and foremost thing for us to do whenever faced with difficulty is to cry out to God.

Dave's Story

Dave was struggling. And part of the problem was that he couldn't put his finger on exactly what the problem was. There were all sorts of things going on for him—worries about redundancy at work, tensions with his wife, concerns about his children—but none of them quite accounted for how he was feeling. Everything seemed like an effort and he found it very difficult to make clear decisions. Someone had told him that he looked depressed and that really wound him up. The last thing he wanted was to be pigeonholed as someone who "couldn't cope" or who "needed help."

So he made a determined effort to put on a brave face, and let everyone know that he was alright. But he knew he wasn't, and acting falsely just troubled him even more. When he was sitting on the bus or when he couldn't sleep at night, he would think these things over and over, with all sorts of ideas bouncing round his head, trying to work out what was really the problem and what to do about it. But it never helped. His thoughts just went round in circles and he ended up thinking that perhaps his problem was that he thought about things too much! The same thing happened when he tried to pray. All these thoughts rattling round, none of them anything like a prayer, but all of them getting in the way. He just couldn't get anything together that remotely seemed like a prayer.

One Sunday after church, Dave ended up chatting with Colin, who ran their home group. After a few minutes, Colin said to him, "Dave, it seems like you're having a rough time of it at the moment." Normally he would have denied it, or made little of it, but this time the question was so gentle and matter-of-fact, Dave felt like he had nothing to lose. "Well, yeah, I am actually." An awkward silence. Dave was expecting at any moment to be

given some "helpful advice" that wouldn't be helpful at all, or have some Bible verse thrown at him
as if it provided an easy answer. It didn't happen.
"Well, I'm sorry to hear that. How are you feeling
about it?" Wow! Dave had spent so long keeping
his feelings to himself that he had somehow become convinced that nobody else could possibly
be interested or care about what was going on for
him. "Well, I dunno, I . . . er . . . , I just feel quite low
about a lot of things . . ."

Dave gradually began to loosen up as he realized
that someone was really listening to him and he
was actually being honest. After they had chatted
for a while, Colin said to Dave, "Where does God fit
into the picture? Has it been possible to pray about
any of this?" Dave had a very simple answer to that:
"No, nothing like it." "Well, I'm not surprised at all.
You know, I find the psalms very helpful when I
can't pray any other way. Some of them are spot-on
when you're feeling down. One hundred thirty and
thirteen are my favorites. See what you think."

So Dave did. It seemed quite a strange thing to do
at first, but he got a Bible out, sat down, and read
Psalm 130 out loud. With some extra bits, just to
make sure God knew what he meant: "*Out of the
depths I cry to you, O Lord. Lord, hear my voice!* 'Cos
you know that I feel lousy and I'm reading this as
a sort of prayer. *Let your ears be attentive to the
voice of my supplications.* I need some help here,
and I know that you are listening even though this
doesn't feel like proper praying . . ." And so on.

It felt like an odd thing to do, but Dave could tell
that it made a difference. He had been honest, hon-

est to God, and he had been heard. The way that he felt mattered, and that meant that *he* mattered. It dawned on him that all the time he had been holding his problems to himself, it was like he had been listening to a voice on his shoulder saying, "You don't matter. You're a loser. You can't cope. You're never going to achieve anything." That voice had been hushed. Praying the psalm had not changed his circumstances at all. It had barely changed his feelings about those circumstances. But it had given him something very significant: it had given him back his dignity.

What Dave discovers in this story is that expressing bad feelings to God is not a faith-*less* thing to do. On the contrary, it is a faith-*ful* thing to do. We believe that God knows us intimately, every secret of our hearts. But we don't often put that belief into practice. We tend to say the things we think we ought to say. We try to pray like the person we think we ought to be, rather than the person we are. But God knows all this. God knows and understands what goes on inside us, even before we open our mouths or turn our thoughts to God. When my children were younger, if one of them came to me looking very coy and saying, "Daddy, I think my chair is broken but I didn't do anything to it," I knew straightaway that she did. Hopefully (on a good day!), I wouldn't be mad at her about it. I would want to mend the chair. But I would also want to mend the relationship: I would invite her to admit that she did break the chair, because there needed to be honesty between us to maintain a healthy, trusting relationship.

Right before God

In the same way, God is not going to be disappointed with us for having bad feelings. Our heavenly Father God probably does want us to be honest about what is inside us when we turn to him, because that is the only way to maintain a healthy, trusting relationship. So the question for us when we are trying to pray in the context of being greatly disturbed is: do we want to "get it right" and so try to pray in some "proper" way, or do we want to maintain healthy and wholesome contact between us and God, which involves being honest about really difficult things? The psalmists with their loud crying to God, and even, as we shall see in chapter three, with their complaints against God, were more concerned to keep up a right relationship with God than with squashing themselves into some ideal of "godliness."

Have you heard the story Jesus told about a man with two sons? He sent them out to work. The first son said he wouldn't go out to work but then did go; the second son said he would go out to work but then didn't (Matthew 21:28–32). It seems to me that neither son really wanted to do what their father told them. The first son was honest about that. He recognized his unwillingness and expressed it. Evidently he then was able to think things through, and decided to do what his father wanted. In contrast, the second son did not truly express how he felt. He denied to his father that he didn't want to work, and in the process possibly denied it to himself also. He put on a pretense of being a dutiful son. But in time his action—to stay at home and not work—was inevitably dictated by his true feelings. Saying what he thought he ought to say didn't do any good.

Jesus told this parable to explain why "sinners" were entering the kingdom of God ahead of "righteous" people. Here again the contrast is quite apparent. On the one hand, there were people who were putting on a face of being "right" and who thereby cut themselves off from the help they needed. On the other hand, there were people who knew that they were remote from God, but were willing to admit this because they wanted to be part of God's kingdom, so they did "repent and believe." In every way, we see that honest expression before God is faithful, reverent, and the path to deepened connection with God.

Is it wrong to feel the way we do?

Is it wrong to feel pain? No. Pain is a normal, healthy reaction. It tells us that something is wrong and gives us the opportunity to do something about it. In the same way, our painful feelings offer us the opportunity to explore carefully what is wrong, but only if we first genuinely feel them, and this involves expressing them.

Oughtn't we to praise God at all times and in all places?

Yes, but that does not exclude lamenting as well. Indeed, part of the very reason for lamenting is to enable us to praise, as we shall explore in chapter eight.

Isn't it a sin to be angry or doubtful or self-pitying?

Jesus himself was angry on at least one occasion (Mark 3:5) because of other people's "hardness of heart." When Thomas doubted the message that Jesus was raised from the dead, he was not rejected but given fresh reason to believe (John 20:25–28).

Isn't our suffering an indication of our sinfulness for which God rightly chastises us?

When Jesus's disciples wanted to explain suffering as caused by sin, Jesus made clear to them that they were on the wrong lines (John 9:1–3). A similar message is dramatically presented in the book of Job.

What right have we to express our discomfort to God?

We are God's children, dearly loved.

What if a time of trial is sent by God for our good, as part of the process of being made perfect in Christ?

Christ himself was made perfect through suffering (Hebrews 2:10), and in the process "offered up prayers and supplications with loud cries and tears" (Hebrews 5:7). In the garden of Gethsemane, he wrestled with his "cup" of suffering and begged God to take it away (Mark 14:33–36).

What about sharing in Christ's sufferings?

As Christ suffered on the cross, he prayed Psalm 22, which vividly expresses desolation and anguish (Matthew 27:46). Sharing in Christ's sufferings may therefore involve sharing in such prayers.

Say It Like It Is

It's time to put these ideas into practice. If you still have some uneasiness about them because of what is frequently taught in church, have a look at some (very brief) answers to those questions in the box. When you are ready, take a look at another example of how a psalm can be helpful to us when we are afflicted by distressing feelings or circumstances. It is a psalm that is full of strong emotion. This time read it aloud as a prayer and see if you can make it your own.

> O Lord, do not rebuke me in your anger,
>   or discipline me in your wrath.
> Be gracious to me, O Lord, for I am languishing;
>   O Lord, heal me, for my bones are shaking
>   with terror.
> My soul also is struck with terror,
>   while you, O Lord—how long?
>
> Turn, O Lord, save my life;
>   deliver me for the sake of your steadfast love.
> For in death there is no remembrance of you;
>   in Sheol who can give you praise?
>
> I am weary with my moaning;
>   every night I flood my bed with tears;
>   I drench my couch with my weeping.
> My eyes waste away because of grief;
>   they grow weak because of all my foes.
>
> Depart from me, all you workers of evil,
>   for the Lord has heard the sound of my
>   weeping.
> The Lord has heard my supplication;
>   the Lord accepts my prayer.
> All my enemies shall be ashamed and struck with
>   terror;
>   they shall turn back, and in a moment be put
>   to shame.

This is the prayer of someone who was in great distress. I found it very helpful once in a spell of prolonged

illness. I invite you to make it your own too. Like most
of the psalms, the details of the issues that lie behind
this psalm are ambiguous, which is helpful to us when
we use it as our own prayer. It does not take too much
imagination to relate the words of the psalm to our
own circumstances.

The first section of the psalm (vv. 1–5) addresses God
directly and asks for help. There is just one verse that
mentions a concern that God might be rebuking or dis-
ciplining, but four verses that appeal to God's character—
"gracious," "steadfast love"—and plead for relief from
trouble. There is no attempt to resolve the uncertainty
about what is the cause of the situation; rather, the psalm
focuses on the expression of distress. Perhaps we can relate to this: at times of suffering it doesn't much help to
engage in discussions about why it is happening. First we
need to simply "get things off our chest."

The second section (vv. 6–7) conveys a haunting
image of groaning and weeping day after day, night
after night. The weariness of long-term suffering is
powerfully put across. That's one of the really bleak
aspects of being "in the depths"—that you can't see an
end to it. Whether you personally are one for weeping
or not, these verses give voice to the burden of such a
situation. It allows you to "cry out" in every sense of
the phrase, with your whole being. Whether we feel
that the problem is "out there" in our circumstances
or "in here" in our feelings, we can use this prayer to
express the anguished longing for some relief.

The final section (vv. 8–10) looks outward and
talks about the "foes" mentioned at the end of verse
7. In chapter seven we will be looking at this topic in
detail. For now it is worth mentioning that the idea of

"enemies" could be taken to refer to absolutely anything that causes distress: people, circumstances, feelings, or thoughts. The important assertion of this psalm is that, even in the midst of anguish, the very reason for expressing that anguish to God is the belief that God can do something about it. You may not feel hopeful—indeed you may identify with the "How long?" of verse 3—but nevertheless it is good to express that despair and darkness alongside the flickering flame of belief in a God who cares and can act.

So in finding a way through the depths, this is the first thing that we can do: we can express ourselves fully and honestly to God. Questions may remain in our minds about the legitimacy of doing so, but the psalms, as part of Scripture, both provide a divine mandate for crying out to God and offer us the words to use. Expressing ourselves openly enables us to hear our own voice and to engage with the reality of how we feel rather than trying to keep it locked away. It therefore frees us up to consider what is actually going on inside us. "What's the matter with me?" This will be the subject of the next chapter.

Summary: So what can I do now?

- Make staying connected with God your top priority, whether your distress is avoidable or not.
- Be completely honest in expressing your emotions and thoughts to God.
- Pray Psalm 6 in relation to the circumstances that trouble you.

CHAPTER 2

"Is it just me . . . ?"

In this chapter . . .

- How to guard against shame.
- How to deal with guilt.
- Why these are not the same.

What's Wrong with Me?

Looking within ourselves in order to give full expression to the depth of our feelings may well cause us to think that the source of our suffering is actually within us. This is an instinctive reaction to suffering that sits alongside the expression of the pain, frustration, and mental anguish that always accompany distress. It yearns for an explanation for suffering and it looks for that explanation in us. Why do we do that? There are certain beliefs that tend to provoke such a response. By recognizing what these beliefs are, we can then see how we can best move on in our prayers from the expression of distress to the exploration of what within us may need to change.

When, despite our best efforts, life simply doesn't seem to be working for us, we might be tempted to say "What's wrong with me?" One belief that might lie behind this reaction to suffering is the sense of there being something fundamentally bad or wrong about us. Yet this belief can be very difficult indeed to recognize. And in actual fact there may be nothing "wrong" with us at all.

In the film *Good Will Hunting*, the title figure, Will Hunting, is a precociously gifted but deeply troubled young man. The result of growing up with an abusive father is that he is alienated from society, often gets into fights, and tends to ruin any opportunities that are offered to him. He is befriended by a college professor who recognizes Will's academic ability and gives him the opportunity to make use of it. The enterprise is considered hopeless by the professor's peers, and they appear to be right as one failure follows another and Will continues to rebel even against those who are trying to help him. But the crucial turning point comes when the professor confronts Will with the reality of what has happened to him and repeats over and over to him, "It's not your fault. It's not your fault. It's not your fault." Will resists initially, but eventually breaks down, and for the first time in his life accepts comfort and love from someone else.

One of the most important things we might need to hear when we are suffering is: "It's not your fault." Will Hunting went through years of his life being hard on himself and punishing himself because he felt bad about who he was. Yet this feeling was not his fault; it was imposed upon him by a parent who nurtured within Will a faulty self-image. The truth of the matter is that, as part of God's creation, there is something inherently good and valuable about all of us. We are not perfect, but God knows and accepts this.

Psalm 139 is very popular and well-known for its depiction of God's intimate knowledge of the psalmist:

O Lord, you have searched me and known me.
  You know when I sit down and when I rise up;
    you discern my thoughts from far away.
  You search out my path and my lying down,
    and are acquainted with all my ways.
  Even before a word is on my tongue,
    O Lord, you know it completely.
        (Psalm 139:1–4)

But we often miss the context in which this meditation on God's knowledge takes place. When we get toward the end of the psalm, we read:

O that you would kill the wicked, O God,
  and that the bloodthirsty would depart
      from me—
those who speak of you maliciously,
  and lift themselves up against you for evil!
        (Psalm 139:19–20)

So here we find that the psalmist is struggling with intensely negative feelings that are born out of mistreatment by others. This is the context in which the psalmist rejoices over God's intimate knowledge! So while the wrestling with painful circumstances is real, there is no suggestion that the psalmist has brought those circumstances upon himself. Rather he goes on to pray that God would reveal whether there is anything wicked in him (vv. 23–24). So this provides us with a model of distinguishing between our distress and anything within us that is not godly.

It is tragic when anybody assumes that their suffering is their own fault. As we see in Will Hunting, this could well be a symptom of a root of shame within them, rather than a reflection of reality. When we find ourselves asking "What's the matter with me?" we need first of all to guard ourselves against distress being a source of shame. The problem is compounded if we have been taught by others—typically parents or other authority figures—that our suffering *is* our own fault. To impose such an idea on a vulnerable person is a form of abuse that can have far-reaching consequences (see Rose's story below). To recognize this is a key step in being able to recover from the harm that it has done.

Feelings of being "bad" or "wrong," unless they are associated with a specific act for which we refuse forgiveness, almost certainly indicate that we have been given a faulty self-image: we see ourselves as a source of shame. This is a very important distinction. God's Holy Spirit does convict us of guilt, so that we can seek forgiveness. But God does not shame people. A feeling that we are inherently worthless or unlovable does not come from God.

So it is important that our prayers affirm this. We are made in the image of God. As part of a fallen world we are not perfect, but we are fully accepted by God in our human frailty.

> For he knows how we are formed,
>   he remembers that we are dust.
>   (Psalm 103:14 NIV)

God is gentle and tolerant, and any sense of inherent unworthiness does not come from God. Unfortunately, the reality of fallen humanity means that even among God's people, this truth has not always been borne out in practice. Luke tells the story of a woman who had suffered from an issue of blood for twelve years (Luke 8:43–48). How could she not have felt shame? Considered ritually "unclean," she would have been shunned, with few if any people willing to touch her. Probably few if any people would ever want her in their house or be willing to share a meal with her. Ostracized by the very community she considered her own, every day of her life would have reinforced the impression that her disease and her value as a person were linked together. Not able even to cry out to Jesus, perhaps for fear of being recognized and publicly shunned in the crowd, she dared to touch his robe. What a shocking thing to do: an "unclean" woman touching a holy man! The power of God's presence in Jesus immediately healed her, not merely restoring her health but affirming her dignity and her place as a member of the community, breaking the supposed link between her value and her well-being. *It wasn't her fault.*

Rose's Story

I have heard the late Selwyn Hughes tell the following story:

Rose had attended church only occasionally during her adult life, and in her later years this ceased altogether. Indeed, she scarcely ventured out at all, and the minister could barely recall when she had last seen Rose when she telephoned one day out of the blue and requested a visit, sounding distressed.

She arranged to visit Rose and did so. It was evident that Rose was suffering the effects of aging, but most noticeable was the disfigurement of her face caused by a mild palsy combined with increasingly patchy pigmentation. They chatted for some time, but Rose found it difficult to make eye contact, and sat with her face turned away for much of the time.

"What prompted you to contact me?" asked the minister, presently.

Rose sighed deeply, then began to speak in a very deliberate, emotionless fashion.

"My mother was very strict. It was always 'Don't do this, don't do that, the Lord knows! He will find you out!' In my teens, I wanted to start wearing makeup, like my friends. 'No makeup!' mother would insist. But I disobeyed, I wore makeup anyway, secretly, without her knowing. And now . . ."

Rose's voice broke and she began to sob. "And now I am being punished. I wanted my face to be pretty. Now God has made it so ugly that I can't show my face to anyone."

Admitting how she felt gave Rose the opportunity for the first time to hear someone else's point of view. The minister was gentle and patient. Over the course of subsequent visits, as they talked about the distress of Rose's disfigurement, the minister would softly repeat "It's not your fault." For Rose, the process of fully accepting God's forgiveness for disobeying her mother went hand in hand with an ability to see that what she suffered was not her own fault. Neither was it God's "punishment."

Walking in Integrity

In view of the importance of separating our distress from our self-worth, some quite remarkable and little-known psalms can be very important prayers for us to use. When we are suffering, the beginning of Psalm 26 can help us to avoid wrongly believing that it's "all our own fault":

> Vindicate me, O LORD,
>   for I have walked in my integrity,
>   and I have trusted in the LORD without
>   wavering.
> Prove me, O LORD, and try me;
>   test my heart and mind.
> For your steadfast love is before my eyes,
>   and I walk in faithfulness to you.
>   (Psalm 26:1–3)

I find the concept of "integrity" hugely helpful here. It conveys a sense of completeness and genuineness. So I don't think the psalm carries a claim of moral perfection. Rather it is the prayer of somebody who is wholehearted in their devotion to God, and who is willing to recognize and seek forgiveness for their sins. So using this psalm as a personal prayer acts as an antidote to any idea that I might be fundamentally bad and therefore be the cause of all my own suffering. It allows me to express to God my desire to do what is good and reminds me that God knows all about me, including the depth of torment and anguish that I might already have been expressing.

So we have seen that issues of self-image are pro-voked by suffering. The psalms that speak of integrity (7, 15, 24, 26) help us to avoid our suffering becoming a source of shame. It may well be the case that *it's not your fault*. But suppose that we are particularly con-scious of our human sinfulness, of the fact that we fall short of God's ways. This can lead us to another belief about suffering: that we are being rightly punished.

What Have I Done to Deserve This?

In times of darkness, we might reasonably find our-selves wondering whether our affliction is a direct con-sequence of our own actions. The book of Deuteronomy in particular described blessings for the righteous and punishment of the wicked. Many of the Old Testament prophets used the same ideas to describe the sufferings of the people of Israel as chastisement from God in light of their unfaithfulness. And even in the New Testament there are some indications that wrong behavior may have fairly immediate and drastic consequences (see Acts 5:1–11). But such thinking can be taken too far if we suppose that all suffering is a direct result of sin.

The book of Job consists principally of a dramatic dialogue between Job and his three friends. Job is a good man who is suffering to an extraordinary degree. His friends insist that this must be an indication of his sin, and urge him to confess his wrongdoing to God. Job counters that he could not possibly deserve the degree of affliction that he is experiencing. He is a man of integrity and, while not perfectly blameless, could not be responsible for such devastating calamity.

At the end of the dialogue, God speaks and vindicates Job's perspective.

So while we recognize that God may use affliction as a chastisement, or a means of "bringing us to our senses," it is vital that we do not see it only in such terms. The Good News of the Christian faith is one of grace—favor freely bestowed—not one of rigid cause and effect. As is asserted in Anglican liturgy, God does *not* treat us as our sins deserve.

This principle can be seen most clearly in the Gospel of John when Jesus is dragged into an argument about whose sin caused a man's blindness. Jesus says, "Neither this man nor his parents sinned; he was born blind so that God's works might be revealed in him" (John 9:3). That is a truly radical perspective. The things we live through that are so testing and difficult may not be intended to highlight shortcomings and failings, but may be means of revealing the glory of God!

A specific illustration of this principle can be found in Psalm 7:

> O Lord my God, if I have done this,
>   if there is wrong in my hands,
> if I have repaid my ally with harm
>   or plundered my foe without cause,
> then let the enemy pursue and overtake me,
>   trample my life to the ground,
>   and lay my soul in the dust.
> The Lord judges the peoples;
>   judge me, O Lord, according to my
>   righteousness
>   and according to the integrity that is in me.
>   (Psalm 7:3–5, 8)

Here the psalmist is concerned with specific deeds that would clearly warrant a response from God for the sake of justice. But the psalmist has *not* done these things. Rather an appeal is made on the basis of the psalmist's integrity.

So when we are in trouble, this psalm, like Psalm 26, can be a fruitful prayer that will help us to keep a clear perspective as we look inward at our discomfort and consider its source. Together they remind us that we are not bad people, and that misfortune is not necessarily our own fault. They set our weaknesses alongside our commitment to God and our efforts to act faithfully and obediently. And they allow us, with Job, to lay before God any sense of disproportion between how we live and what we suffer.

Equally, the psalms' protestations of integrity and innocence may prick our conscience and highlight areas of our lives that are not as God would want them to be. The psalm which cries "out of the depths" also meditates on the human need for forgiveness and God's forgiving nature:

> If you, O Lord, should mark iniquities,
>   Lord, who could stand?
> But there is forgiveness with you,
>   so that you may be revered. (Psalm 130:3–4)

In the light of this assurance of forgiveness with God, let's look at how personal acknowledgement of weaknesses and failings can help us to pray.

Have Mercy on Me, O God

Suppose now that our self-appraisal, guided by the Holy Spirit, highlights attitudes or actions for which we need forgiveness. How does God forgive? Psalm 51 is highly useful in establishing a pattern for the practice of confession and an understanding of the process through which a damaged relationship with God can be restored. We saw in the previous chapter how the process of expressing true feelings was vital in order to maintain a healthy relationship with God. Similarly now we can think of forgiveness as an interaction between a believer and God that restores the relationship when it has been damaged. Since it is God who forgives, the prayer for forgiveness is made on the basis of God's steadfast love, reminding us again that God looks favorably on those who seek him, and is concerned to forgive, not to blame.

> Have mercy on me, O God,
>> according to your steadfast love;
> according to your abundant mercy
>> blot out my transgressions. (Psalm 51:1)

The psalm begins with the assertion that God is merciful, a God who forgives sins. It appeals to the full breadth of God's gracious and forgiving character. There are two separate words translated "mercy," one referring to God's gracious kindness and one to God's compassion. The appeal to God's steadfast love speaks of God's willing and deliberate faithfulness toward those whom he has chosen and saved. Thus the psalm appeals as broadly as possible to the caring and forgiving nature of God.

The breadth of appeal to God's character leads to an even broader confession of those aspects of the psalmist's condition and behavior for which forgiveness is sought.

> For I know my transgressions,
>   and my sin is ever before me.
> Against you, you alone, have I sinned,
>   and done what is evil in your sight.
>   (Psalm 51:3–4a)

Despite the superscription of the psalm (ascribing it to David after his adultery with Bathsheba) the nature of the sin is not explicitly mentioned. But because of this, we can use the psalm as a pattern for any confession. Indeed, the three separate words for wrongdoing that are used give the psalm a very broad scope. "Transgressions" implies the willful violation of an accepted norm, the rebellion against an authority and hence a deliberate breach of trust. "Sin" is broader and has a sense of "missing the mark" or failing in some manner. It may not therefore be deliberate but conveys the weakness of human nature. "Evil" is broader still in the original language and might better be translated as "bad." It encompasses all those things that we might think of as "unhelpful," "unfortunate," or "foolish," rather than "wrong" in a strictly moral sense. So the psalm assures us that God can, and does, forgive not only our willful disobedience and not only our weaknesses and failings, but even any aspects of our lives that are "bad" either for God or for us or for other people.

The significance of specific words or actions in enacting that forgiveness comes in the following verses:

Purge me with hyssop, and I shall be clean;
    wash me, and I shall be whiter than snow.
Let me hear joy and gladness;
    let the bones that you have crushed rejoice.
        (Psalm 51:7–8)

The reference to hyssop invokes the instructions given by God (in Leviticus 14 and Numbers 19) for rituals of purification. It reminds us that God's forgiveness is a concrete reality. Whether or not we feel any different, we can be confident that once God has forgiven, that is the end of the matter. As my friends in Africa say: God takes our sins and casts them into the deep, deep lake, where there is also a sign, "No Fishing!" When sins are gone, they are gone for good! Nevertheless, we may need some assurance of this, and a pronouncement of forgiveness can be very helpful, as hinted at by the psalmist's "Let me hear. . . ." For this reason, when we are troubled with a sense of guilt, it can be most helpful to make a specific confession in the presence of others, and to receive an assurance of forgiveness.

The prayer for forgiveness in the psalm leads to a prayer for restoration, since the psalmist knows that having been forgiven, he needs rebuilding, as it were, into a godly person, since he cannot do good by his own efforts.

Create in me a clean heart, O God,
    and put a new and right spirit within me.
Do not cast me away from your presence,
    and do not take your holy spirit from me.
Restore to me the joy of your salvation,
    and sustain in me a willing spirit.
        (Psalm 51:10–12)

The purpose of confession is clearly seen here to be a restored relationship with God. But only God can accomplish this ("create" is a verb of which only God is ever the subject), and so this is the psalmist's plea. The psalmist appeals to be restored to the ongoing experience of God's life-giving, empowering presence.

Psalm 51 thereby sets out a useful pattern for the content and purpose of a confession of guilt, actively bringing about restoration of a relationship with God.

Naming, not shaming.

Make a list of the things that are causing you distress: circumstances, people, disease, difficulties, feelings. What reaction does this provoke in you? Do you feel able to name these things before God, or do you feel embarrassed by any of them? Are there things that you would rather hide, or hide yourself from?

On a separate piece of paper, write or draw something that represents your value as a person, loved and accepted by God.

Now pray Psalm 139 with both pieces of paper out in the open. Focus on God's precious care for you that is not affected or diminished by what you are suffering.

Whose fault is it anyway?

Explore whether you feel responsible for any aspect of the situation that you find yourself in. Remember, you are not looking for perfection in yourself. Have other people ever placed expectations on you that were not reasonable?

Use Psalm 26 as a prayer that expresses your sense of integrity, while being open to the conviction of the Holy Spirit regarding anything that needs God's forgiveness.

Have mercy on me, O God.

If there are things that you feel need to be put right between you and God, consider the pattern of confession and forgiveness described in Psalm 51. You can make the best use of this: either praying in private with a trusted friend or minister, or in the context of corporate worship.

"God goes around mending things that are broken."

This is one of my favorite descriptions of God, and it reminds us that where things have gone wrong in our lives, God is ready to put them right, if we are willing. It also brings to mind the well-known phrase, "If it ain't broke, don't fix it!" By that principle, we need not be blaming ourselves for our troubles when they are not our fault, nor asking again for forgiveness of things from the past that God has already forgiven.

In this chapter we have seen how we can guard our worth and dignity with the prayers that assert our integrity. We have reminded ourselves that suffering is not to be equated with punishment and that where we are aware of attitudes or actions that come between us and God, Psalm 51 gives us a pattern for confessing and receiving forgiveness. The suggestions in the box will help you to apply these principles for yourself.

But what if all this soul-searching doesn't help very much? What if in fact it seems like it is God who is the problem—allowing our trouble in the first place and failing to answer our prayers? Then what? In the next chapter, we begin to look beyond ourselves and dare to ask questions of God.

Summary: So what can I do now?

- Remember that God knows and accepts your frailty (Psalm 103:14).
- Focus on grace: God does not treat us according to what we deserve.
- Use the suggestions for prayer in the box above.

CHAPTER 3

". . . OR HAS GOD GONE?"

In this chapter . . .

- How to deal with doubt in God.
- How to complain to God.
- Why this is a faithful way to relate to God.

When Faith Is Hard to Find

We have explored together the importance of being able to give full voice to our feelings, no matter what they may be, in the context of our relationship with God. And we have particularly examined how using the psalms of confession can help us both to make changes within ourselves (should that be necessary) and to guard against false guilt and shame. Our troubles may not be our own fault at all. So whose fault are they?

Consider this situation: A man who has been very active in the church for most of his life, often in a position of leadership, contracts cancer. He is well supported by the church and many are praying for him, but his suffering gradually increases. The faith he has followed starts to crumble. How can God allow this? Why him? He becomes very low-spirited and no longer feels able to pray. Attending church makes him feel hypocritical, and so he ceases to do so. Many are shocked and disheartened by this apparent loss of faith in one they had looked up to.

Or this situation: A woman in her thirties, who has been brought up in a strong church family, is struggling with parenthood. She is questioning many things she had taken for granted. As her children ask her about what goes on in church, and her non-Christian friends criticize religion, she also questions her own Christian assumptions and feels her faith being undermined. She feels both confused and angry with God and no longer knows how to pray.

These stories illustrate some of the ways in which suffering can undermine faith. This is compounded when your faith, or "the church," is a contributing factor. Indeed, when it comes down to it, we may well feel as if it is God who is the source of our trouble. Faced with such a situation, I have seen people take one of two paths. One is to give up on God altogether: to bring an end to their journey of faith and walk away from God, and therefore the church. The other is to harbor a sense of blame against God for the pain but never expressing it, such that it poisons an ongoing relationship with God. Is there another way?

Without Faith

Is it possible to pray without faith? I believe it is, but ironically the important thing is not to ignore what bit of faith we do have. A hospital chaplain was ministering to a lady who had severe health problems. The treatment had a good chance of success, but she was in considerable discomfort for quite some time. The chaplain sat with her and chatted with her comfortably, but was rebuffed whenever he suggested praying. As he gently questioned why this was the case, the lady somewhat bitterly catalogued the ways in which she felt forgotten by God and hurt by people in the church. So the chaplain did a remarkable thing. He got hold of an old stained glass window and set it up against a wall around the outside of the hospital. He took the lady out there and put stones in her hands and said, "This window represents the church which represents God. So you go ahead. Throw the stones and smash the window. Take your anger out on God." The lady broke down and could not. But she was then ready to pray.

That lady was ignoring God because she could not admit how angry she felt toward him. Anger has a habit of doing that: if we can't find a way to express it, then we tend to avoid or ignore the people with whom we are angry. This applies to God just as much as to other people, and I suspect that feelings of frustration, betrayal, and abandonment have much the same effect. What might seem like a "loss of faith" often conceals a burden of negative feelings that are inhibiting a relationship with God.

Take that!

If you feel that you want to give up on God, or are despairing, try to explore whether you are in fact feeling let down or angry with God. If so, consider whether you might find a way to express that to God, rather than turning away.

Whatever your situation, if you have any awareness of being angry with God, a powerful exercise is to express that by banging some nails into a piece of wood. In some sense this provides a "safe" outlet for a very strong feeling. It also grounds us in the reality of the fact that, in the crucifixion of Jesus, God has already literally been on the receiving end of such action. It reminds us that Jesus carries the pain and the sin of the world, and provides the means for our restoration and healing. The way through this is to find a way to express the reality of the situation *within* the relationship. On extreme occasions I have found myself praying a prayer along the lines of: "Dear God, I'm not sure I believe in you anymore." I have dared to do this because it matches the shockingly strident language that we find in the psalms.

Several of the psalms offer forthright complaint to God about situations that are regarded as God's responsibility. Psalm 44 is the prayer of people whose trust in God has seemingly led them to ruin. It has become particularly associated in modern times with the Holocaust. It begins with apparent praise (vv. 1–8), recounting God's faithful and generous dealings with his people in the past:

> We have heard with our ears, O God,
>   our ancestors have told us,
> what deeds you performed in their days,
>   in the days of old. (Psalm 44:1)

But the tenor of the psalm changes dramatically with the disjunction that opens verse 9:

> Yet you have rejected us and abased us,
>   and have not gone out with our armies.
> You made us turn back from the foe,
>   and our enemies have gotten spoil.

You have made us like sheep for slaughter,
    and have scattered us among the nations.
You have sold your people for a trifle,
    demanding no high price for them.

You have made us the taunt of our neighbors,
    the derision and scorn of those around us.
You have made us a byword among the nations,
    a laughingstock among the peoples.
All day long my disgrace is before me,
    and shame has covered my face
at the words of the taunters and revilers,
    at the sight of the enemy and the avenger.
        (Psalm 44:9–16)

Here is a whole series of complaints against God: *You* made us turn back, *You* have made us like sheep for the slaughter, *You* have sold your people, *You* have made us the taunt of our neighbors. This is strong language indeed, laying the blame for the pitiful plight of the people squarely at God's door. It then becomes apparent that the opening verses of praise are in fact rather pointed, perhaps even ironic, serving to sharpen the complaints that follow. It is precisely because of God's faithfulness in the past that the people have such cause for complaint now.

The concluding section of the psalm brings these themes together to address directly the discord between God's promises and God's apparent neglect.

Rouse yourself! Why do you sleep, O Lord?
    Awake, do not cast us off forever!
Why do you hide your face?

> Why do you forget our affliction and oppres-
> sion? (Psalm 44:23–24)

Similar questions and accusations can be found in other psalms too. The immediate cause of suffering may be persecution/humiliation by other people, sickness, or other physical threat. But according to the psalmists, it is the silence of God that allows enemies to speak evil and weakness in the face of evil is due to God "hiding his face." Since God can influence the actions of other people, the troublesome circumstances could be prevented by God—but are not.

Therefore in each case a strong complaint is laid against God in the context of prayer. God is accused of abandoning, rejecting, sleeping, neglecting, and forgetting. The image of God turning away or hiding his face is particularly poignant, suggesting the breakdown of a relationship and the experience of the psalmist that it is God who is responsible for this.

How Dare You!

It is worth pausing at this point to consider our reaction to the idea of making complaints against God, or asking searching questions of God, in prayer. Perhaps the idea is unsettling or even shocking. If so, I would invite you to explore whether aspects of our spiritual traditions have contributed to this. Such psalms of complaint have not always been well regarded through the history of the church. In the early centuries, St. Augustine taught a spirituality that emphasized personal confession of sin, placing the responsibility for human suffering squarely on human sinfulness. At the time of the Reformation, John Calvin wrote of the importance of patient endurance through difficulties, emphasizing the virtues of submission and perseverance. These trains of thought are still influential in the church today, and may well inhibit us from using the psalms of complaint. Phrases such as "If you feel far away from God, guess who moved!" may be motivated by a desire to promote godly living, but for the person who *feels* abandoned by God, they simply add insult to injury.

So at this point we must make an important distinction between expression of feelings and statements of truth. When the psalmists prayed in times of distress, they were not trying to offer a "true" picture of who God is. Rather they were allowing their understanding of God to influence the way in which they expressed their experiences, thoughts, and feelings at that particular time.

This important point might be clearer if we consider the opposite possibility: that there may be no legitimate complaint against God. To what might such a relationship be compared? The dictator who violently puts down anyone who opposes him and the people facing daily injustice and oppression who may pay with their lives if they speak out. The boss at work who makes increasingly onerous demands and the staff who risk getting fired if they step out of line. The marriage where one partner is "always right," reacting angrily and withdrawing love whenever challenged, while the other partner constantly tries to "keep the peace" at considerable cost to themselves. The parent imposing unreasonable expectations and the children who dare not object for fear of punishment. In all these scenarios a relationship that is essentially abusive, at some level, is characterized by the inability of one party to voice their complaint. Is that what a relationship with God should be like? I am certain that it is not. Rather we may think of God as a good ruler who tolerates his subjects' complaints, as a good partner who is willing to respond to the other, and as a good parent who understands and accepts the children's frustrations and need for nurture.

When I was preparing to be married, I received all sorts of advice, not all of which was asked for! It is almost all long since forgotten, save for one particular comment that sticks in mind: "Make sure that you tell your partner anything you are unhappy about." That advice had a profound and lasting impact. It was in no way a mandate to moan from a selfish point of view, or to make the other person feel bad, or to think that I should get everything my own way. Rather it recognized that, personally, I had a habit of *not* talking about the things I found difficult. I had a tendency to try to put up with them, under the impression that this was good for the relationship. In actual fact, holding back was definitely *bad* for the relationship, because I was not genuinely being a part of it. It has been my experience that being able to complain, and being willing to receive complaints, is vital to any healthy relationship.

As a means of relating to God, the psalms provide examples of prayers of complaint. In their origin they provided the means for the people of Israel to keep going in their worship and service of God, even when they felt abandoned or let down by God. So too we can make the prayers our own when we feel that we are in similar circumstances.

I Thought You Loved Me

What we are discovering is that a willingness to complain is not a sign of a weak or one-sided relationship. On the contrary, it indicates the outworking of a strong mutual relationship, where each party is respected and afforded dignity by the other. It is in the context of the past relationship with God that the psalmists formed their prayers. This was particularly in evidence in Psalm 44, which opens with a recollection of God's saving acts of the past. It is precisely because the psalmist understands that God has drawn people into a covenant relationship, and the psalmist has experienced (or at least heard about) the benefits of this, that he now questions so stridently what has changed. Indeed, the psalms at times ask very provocative questions—"Why do you sleep, O Lord?"—and make demands—"Rouse yourself!"—based upon the firm conviction of God's power to respond and historic commitment to do so.

Whenever people use such psalms as their prayer, they are therefore taking God's character and covenant, as revealed through the Scriptures, with the utmost seriousness. They do so very much within the context of relationship. In the case of Psalm 44 there is a clear link with the idea of integrity that we looked at in the previous chapter.

All this has come upon us,
  yet we have not forgotten you,
  or been false to your covenant.
Our heart has not turned back,
  nor have our steps departed from your way,

> yet you have broken us in the haunt of jackals,
>   and covered us with deep darkness.
>   (Psalm 44:17–19)

Here we see that the complaining against God is set in the context of relationship and the psalmist is clear that the people have played their part rightly. They may not be perfect, but they have sought to live out the covenant with God in the way they live their lives. All of this should reassure us that we can legitimately use the psalms of complaint as appropriate forms of prayer when we feel that God is responsible for our distress, either by action or neglect. It is vital that in such circumstances we do not give up on God, nor ignore the reality of our situation. Rather we can with confidence voice the pain and frustration of a seemingly faltering relationship within the context of that relationship.

You Have Put Me in the Depths

Psalm 88 is a powerful example of a psalm of complaint. It particularly addresses feelings of abandonment and of being cut off from other people. It may have particular resonance for someone who has been bereaved or for someone who is losing their faith. The figurative nature of the language invites us to use our imagination and relate to it from our own personal perspective. I suggest that you read it through in full in a Bible, noting the following aspects.

> You have put me in the depths of the Pit,
>   in the regions dark and deep.

Your wrath lies heavy upon me,
   and you overwhelm me with all your waves.
      (Psalm 88:6–7)

The first section uses the language of death. "Sheol" and "the Pit" are two Hebrew terms that are used to describe the underworld, the place that represented death. It is the place of darkness, of nonexistence, where people were figuratively thought to "go" when they died. So the psalmist here is saying, "I feel close to death," or, perhaps, "this situation is so bad I might as well be dead." The psalm expresses the feeling that it is God who has brought this about. Since God is the only one who can create and sustain life, God is held responsible for the deathly situation in which the psalmist finds himself. Similarly, when we are faced with a "fate worse than death," we may need to voice to God our sense of being overwhelmed and of God's hand in that.

But I, O Lord, cry out to you;
   in the morning my prayer comes before you.
O Lord, why do you cast me off?
   Why do you hide your face from me?
      (Psalm 88:13–14)

Here we have a strong sense of the complaint to God being made in the context of a relationship. As difficult as it might be, the psalmist is trying not to give up on God and describes the weariness of crying out for help day after day. We can only speculate about the range of moods—hope, pain, frustration, despair—that he must have been going through. So why is nothing happening? Where is God and what is God doing? The silence of unanswered prayer is poignantly described as the "hiding" of God's face. There is a sense of God being the one who is giving up on the relationship, not the psalmist. I fully sympathize with anyone who has given up praying because it seemed like God was ignoring them. But here is a more positive alternative: to complain to God. All the hurt and frustration can be expressed within the relationship and by offering it as a prayer, allowed to facilitate a sense of connection with God rather than detract from it.

> Your wrath has swept over me;
>> your dread assaults destroy me.
> They surround me like a flood all day long;
>> from all sides they close in on me.
> You have caused friend and neighbor to shun me;
>> my companions are in darkness.
>> (Psalm 88:16–18)

The closing of the psalm describes an experience in terms of being assaulted by God and of being cut off from others. This may well reflect our own experience of how physical, emotional, and social aspects of suffering often go hand in hand. Sometimes it seems as if everything keeps going wrong. The issues we are struggling with have an adverse effect on our family life and friendships, and vice versa. We can end up feeling as if someone, or something, is conspiring against us. When I was ill for an extended period, one of the most difficult aspects of it was that I had no contact with friends or colleagues. Yet the principal issue was my physical illness. Conversely, my experiences of bereavement have been that it has an effect

on me physically, making me very tired or even un-
well. As the psalm provides the means for us to voice
our pain to God, it is important that we can include
every aspect of our affliction: physical, emotional, and
social. We recognize that the whole of our being matters, and even as we voice such negative thoughts about
our circumstances, we are actually affirming our belief
(however slight) that God does indeed care about the
whole of our being too.

Learning to Complain

I conclude this chapter with a personal reflection
on the process of learning to complain. For me, it has
not come naturally. My upbringing fostered in me an
attitude of "putting up" with things rather than voicing
any dissatisfaction. While this generated resilience, it
also resulted in a very limited ability to complain where
it would have been appropriate to do so. Where I did
come across explicit complaining—perhaps in television dramas or in my early career on building sites—it
was usually associated with fierce anger and had quite
a destructive aspect to it. So the only modes of relating
that I was familiar with were ignoring discomfort (and
carrying the burden of it), or exploding in rage. Both
of these are detrimental to good relationships.

I learned a very different way from a colleague at
work. I would occasionally overhear him on the tele-
phone using phrases such as, "I am very unhappy with
the service you have provided," or "That is not an ac-
ceptable outcome," or "You have clearly not dealt with
me reasonably." What made an impact on me was that

these comments were being made clearly and calmly. There was no hiding from them, nor was there any great drama or invective. There was certainly emotion in them, and when he was annoyed it was evident that this was so. But the key aspect was that his complaints were being voiced in a positive manner, in order to preserve and restore his relationship, be it personal or professional, with the other person.

So I am well aware that I have had to learn how to complain. I have moved from seeing it as something dangerous to something very beneficial, when done well. I see in the psalms examples of it being done well, and it is in using the psalms in my own life that I have gone on learning. I encourage you to do the same.

There are more things for us to learn from the psalms too. As we move on from thinking about voicing our complaints to God, the next step is to consider how we then form our prayers so that God will respond. Does it matter how we pray? Can we influence God? This will be the topic of the next chapter.

Summary: So what can I do now?

- Tell God what you think about him, including doubts and anger.
- Aim to strengthen your relationship with God by being accountable and holding God to account.
- Practice complaint that avoids aggression and that seeks restoration.

CHAPTER 4

"I NEED HELP HERE!"

In this chapter . . .

- How to ask for help.
- How to provoke God's compassion.
- Why you can do so.

God Can Help

We have looked quite carefully into the subject of complaining to God, and although this might seem uncomfortable in principle, there are at least two good reasons for doing so: that we actually feel let down by God, and that God as the ultimate authority over the world can potentially make our situation different, no matter what type of difficulty we find ourselves in.

This second reason—God's ultimate authority and potential to change things for the better—leads us to think about the process of asking God to do something. We have cried out to God in the belief that God cares about us and in the belief that God can potentially change things for the better. This is naturally followed by our asking God to do just that.

I would imagine that most of us are on more familiar ground here. Indeed, for many people "praying" means virtually the same thing as "asking God for something." Many church prayer meetings comprise simply of a list of things to ask God for, and the "intercessions" (which means pleas or requests) are often referred to as the "prayers," as if these are one and the same thing. For the rest of this chapter, I will refer to such prayer as "petition." This makes a careful distinction of the type of prayer that we are considering, and has some helpful aspects to it, which we shall explore shortly.

Despite our familiarity with petitionary prayer, there are some curious questions about it that few people have stopped to consider:

Why do we make petitions to God?

Is the likelihood of God doing something affected by our asking?

Does that mean that we are influencing God?

And if so, does it make any difference *how* we make our petitions?

By making petitions to God we are indicating our belief that God can be influenced by our prayers. It may seem surprising to put it in those terms, but it is clearly the case if we consider the opposite. Suppose that God was beyond all influence, that the way God responded to what happens in the world could not be affected by anyone's prayers. Why then would we ask God anything? It would be futile. So our willingness to enter into petitionary prayer demonstrates an instinctive belief and hope in us that God can be influenced by our prayer. There is a good biblical basis for this, which we will consider shortly, but first let's consider for a moment how people ask for what they want.

Pretty Please

Let's think first about a child asking something of a parent. We may well know, or can at least imagine, that the *manner* in which the child asks has an effect on the parent, and consequently on the parent's response. A child may ask on a whim, or carelessly. A child may ask only once or without any indication of a reason for the request. None of these ways are likely to have a particular influence on a parent. Indeed, as an aside, I have found myself as a parent sometimes saying "Ask me properly" to my children. I want them to have what they want, but I also want them to ask in a good manner!

Conversely, a child can ask in a manner that is much more persuasive. They may think carefully about what they want and present not only a request but also reasons for the request. They may well appeal to something that their parent has said or suggested in the past. And if it really matters to them, they will ask more than once. This sort of asking is much more likely to produce a response from a parent.

The same principle applies to adult relationships. Whether in a family, at work, or in church, the manner with which requests are made has significant bearing on the likely response. Consider what has an influence on you personally. What factors make you more likely to respond to a request? For me, I know that an explanation of the reasons for the request is vital. I feel that I need to understand the need and the situation behind it before I will consider responding. An out-of-context "Please will you do this?" does not generate any particular willingness, but leaves me asking, "Why?"

So if the manner of asking is significant in human relationships, is the same true of making petitions to God? Some remarkable stories that Jesus told suggest that it is true. In Luke 18:1–8 Jesus tells of a widow who is being denied justice by the negligence of a judge who could not be bothered to attend to her. Eventually he does respond out of weariness at her continual requests. Jesus then makes a direct comparison between God and the judge in the story, saying, "Will not God grant justice to his chosen ones who cry to him day and night?" On the one hand this suggests that God is more likely to respond than the unjust judge of the story, and this is very reassuring for those of us who depend on God. On the other hand, it also suggests that God's response is bound up with the ongoing cries of God's people, and that their persistence in prayer is a vital aspect of God's working in the world. Indeed, Luke in his retelling of the story tells us the "point" of the story even before it begins: "Jesus told them a parable about their need to pray always and not to lose heart."

The Art of Persuasion

Persistence in prayer is encouraged as something that influences God's response and involvement in human affairs, and it seems reasonable to me that other aspects of persuasion are equally valid. This is the significance of referring to "petition": that it implies the construction of a persuasive argument for God to respond, not merely a simple request. At its heart, such persuasion is rooted in an ongoing relationship with God and the promises that God has made in drawing people into relationship.

We have already looked at Psalm 6 as a model of crying out to God. Let's turn to it again, to see in more detail the way it crafts persuasive arguments for God to respond.

> Be gracious to me, O LORD, for I am languishing;
>> O LORD, heal me, for my bones are shaking
>>> with terror.
> My soul also is struck with terror,
>> while you, O LORD—how long?
>
> Turn, O LORD, save my life;
>> deliver me for the sake of your steadfast love.
> For in death there is no remembrance of you;
>> in Sheol who can give you praise?
>>> (Psalm 6:2–5)

This is a very emotive plea from someone who is suffering terribly. The exact nature of their affliction is not known, but it is described as affecting them physically. It might be a physical illness, or as we noted in the previous chapter, it may be emotional distress or insecurity that affects the psalmist so strongly that it manifests itself in physical ways. The ambiguity over the original situation means that we can make this our own prayer in all sorts of different circumstances.

Notice how an emotional appeal is constructed to move God to compassionate action. The plea for help and relief is bracketed by descriptions of how terrible the psalmist feels. The clear implication is that God should be moved by pity to help someone in such distress. Appeal is also made to God's "steadfast love," bringing to the fore the faithfulness of God that is so often spoken about in the Bible. The reminder of God's own faithfulness is set in contrast to the preceding agonized question "How long?" In effect the psalmist is saying "Why are you taking so long to help me when you have revealed yourself as a God of compassion and faithfulness?" In fact the desolate cry of verse 3 is as powerful for what it does not say as for what it does. It seems to be cut short, allowing us to give it our own particular meaning. How long will you neglect me? How long I have suffered! How long until I find relief? It can be read as question, as accusation, as exclamation. It disturbs and provokes a response.

It does not end there, however, and seemingly faced with the real possibility of death, the psalmist asks "in Sheol (the world of the dead) who can give you praise?" The significance of praise is that it forms the bedrock of a right relationship between God and people. The fundamental way in which we relate to God is by giving him praise. So why should God allow that to come to a premature end? The psalmist is here appealing to the relationship that, as one of God's people, he has been called into by God. That relationship is valuable to God as well as to the psalmist, and the psalmist reminds God of this in order to move him to act.

In the last chapter we saw how the psalms legitimate our cries to God of "Don't I matter to you? Why are you letting this happen?" So now we see that the psalms also provide the pattern for us to persuade God to act, with petitions such as "I *do* matter to you—that's why you saved me. So act as if I matter! Take care of me!" Such a focus on the relationship between God and the believer is even more explicit in another example, this time from Psalm 85.

> Lord, you were favorable to your land;
>   you restored the fortunes of Jacob.
> You forgave the iniquity of your people;
>   you pardoned all their sin.
> You withdrew all your wrath;
>   you turned from your hot anger.
>
> Restore us again, O God of our salvation,
>   and put away your indignation toward us.
> Will you be angry with us forever?
>   Will you prolong your anger to all
>   generations?
> Will you not revive us again,
>   so that your people may rejoice in you?
> Show us your steadfast love, O Lord,
>   and grant us your salvation. (Psalm 85:1–7)

Again the circumstances are not clear, but the psalmist begins this prayer by bringing to mind, and to God's attention, an occasion in the past when God acted favorably toward the people of Israel (described here poetically as "Jacob"). The things that the people had suffered were interpreted as a sign of God's displeasure and therefore God's favor and restoration were interpreted as a sign of pardon of the people's sins. This is a strongly relational way of understanding how God interacts with people. There is nothing static or automatic here. Rather there is a dynamic relationship between parties with strong thoughts, feelings, and motivations.

Therefore the people put their petitions to God in the context of this relationship and seek to persuade God to again act favorably toward them. God has done so in the past, why shouldn't he do so again now? No doubt the people have in mind the stories of all the times that God rescued Israel: from slavery in Egypt and from numerous threats of foreign invasion. Through it all God was held to be a God of steadfast love, as indeed God was first revealed to Moses,

> "The LORD, the LORD
> a God merciful and gracious,
> slow to anger,
> and abounding in steadfast love and faithfulness,
> keeping steadfast love for the thousandth
>   generation,
> forgiving iniquity and transgression and sin,
> yet by no means clearing the guilty,
> but visiting the iniquity of the parents
> upon the children
> and the children's children,
> to the third and the fourth generation."
>   (Exodus 34:6–7)

Even though this self-revelation of God describes the effects of sin being carried by four generations, this stands in stark contrast to the steadfast love and faithfulness that extends to a *thousand* generations. It is with such a revelation of God in mind that the people appeal to God's faithfulness, seeking prosperity and security under God's hand.

What Shall We Pray For?

Given that we are exploring how to create persuasive prayers—giving God reasons to act, relying on an ongoing relationship with God, and appealing to God's character—the question arises as to what we should actually ask God for. The figurative and emotive language of the psalms can be very helpful for us insofar as it is nonspecific, but the actual details for what the psalmists asked of God are not necessarily going to be appropriate for us to ask in turn.

That is because we are in a different context from the psalmists and relate to God in a different way. Jesus reinterpreted what the kingdom of God would be like, and made clear that the story of God's salvation was going to be worked out in a manner that the ancient psalm-writers might have found rather surprising. The headings in the box explore some of the key areas where a Christian perspective will need to adapt some of the thinking evident in the psalms.

Pray for . . . peace and security?

The psalmists would have wanted this in political terms for the ancient nation of Israel. However, as Christians we know that the kingdom of God is not related to a specific place or national group. Indeed, Jesus taught his followers that their allegiance to the kingdom of God would bring them into conflict with worldly authorities and may provoke hostility.

Therefore our prayers for peace and security need to bear this in mind. It is right that we should seek God's protection from trouble or harm, but we also need to remember that troubles will come and Jesus never promised anyone they would be spared the effects of living in a broken world. We do need to pray for the strength to endure our difficulties, as well as asking God for relief from them.

Pray for . . . prosperity?

Many of the psalms seek God's abundant provision, and indeed the success or failure of harvests was often seen as an indication of God's favor or punishment. Jesus taught about the dangers of relying on riches because of their potential to distract people from devotion to God. Instead he taught his followers to pray that God would meet their daily needs. Similarly, Paul wrote to Christians encouraging them to be content with what they had.

So while it is good that we should present our needs to God, we need to be wary of thinking that God can be persuaded to give us everything we want—not least because that might not be very good for us!

Pray for . . . judgment?

The psalms often seek God's judgment on those who do wrong and oppose God's ways. This is related to an understanding of justice being needed in the world, and God being the only and rightful enactor of justice.

As we use the psalms for prayer, we need to remember that God's judgment is deferred until the final day when Jesus returns and God's authority is fully implemented. On that day, all those who have remained faithful to God will be vindicated. In the meantime there is a struggle between good and evil, and our prayers might involve us in that struggle. We will consider this more fully in chapter seven.

Let's now look at another example of a petitionary psalm, noting both what the prayer is for and the reasons that are given for God to respond. This may then become a pattern for our own prayer.

Because I Am Your Servant

Hear my prayer, O LORD;
    give ear to my supplications in your
        faithfulness;
    answer me in your righteousness.
Do not enter into judgment with your servant,
    for no one living is righteous before you.
        (Psalm 143:1–2)

This psalm is focused almost entirely on the psalmist's need for God's help in a condition of desperation due to his "enemies." The psalmist admits that, terrible as his condition is, the prospect of being judged by God is far more terrible. He knows that he cannot be justified according to his own merits, and therefore relies entirely upon the grace of God, seeking help even though he cannot justify his cause from any righteousness of his own. Therefore, right at the outset God's faithfulness and righteousness are appealed to, and almost the whole of the second half of the psalm consists of petitions and motivations.

The plea to be spared judgment might indicate that the sufferings of the psalmist, while superficially due to his enemies, are actually felt to be God's punishment for sin. But what is certain is that the psalmist feels distanced from God as a result of his distress. His sole appeal to God for help implies also that it is God alone who, up to this point, has not been helping him. The psalmist feels humiliated, cut off from God and alienated from society.

> Answer me quickly, O Lord;
>   my spirit fails.
> Do not hide your face from me,
>   or I shall be like those who go down to
>   the Pit.
> Let me hear of your steadfast love in the
>   morning,
>   for in you I put my trust.
> Teach me the way I should go,
>   for to you I lift up my soul.
>
> Save me, O Lord, from my enemies;
>   I have fled to you for refuge.
> Teach me to do your will,
>   for you are my God.
> Let your good spirit lead me
>   on a level path.
>
> For your name's sake, O Lord, preserve my life.
>   In your righteousness bring me out of
>   trouble.
> In your steadfast love cut off my enemies,
>   and destroy all my adversaries,
>   for I am your servant. (Psalm 143:7–12)

In verse 7, the psalmist uses language we have seen elsewhere to say that unless God helps him, he is as good as dead. The plea for God to respond "quickly" may indicate that the psalmist is now at the very end of his tether. It is the eleventh hour, so to speak, and he is desperate for God to act. Where is God in the midst of such distress?

The petitions of the psalmist are variously: for a personal hearing (v. 7), for a response (v. 8a), for guidance (vv. 8b, 10a), for rescue (vv. 9, 11, 12), for protection (v. 10b) and for vindication (v. 12). In this range is evident the extent to which the psalmist's relationship with God is intertwined with his plight at the hands of enemies. The need for guidance, the daily provision of God's grace, is inseparable from the need for rescue from the immediate physical threat.

The main theme of the motivational clauses is one of covenantal faithfulness, based on the phrases: "you are my God" (v. 10) and "I am your servant" (v. 12). The psalmist is seeking to draw God back to the fundamental basis of their relationship, to their identities as sovereign God and chosen people. He reminds God that God has no reputation apart from that of the psalmist. Hence the appeal is made "for your name's sake" (v. 11). Whereas the psalm began with an admission that the psalmist has no merit of his own, it closes with a tacit claim to God's protection on the basis of God's action in drawing the psalmist into covenant relationship. What God has started and promised, he is held to account to finish and fulfill. In the words of Artur Weiser, "The psalmist need not rely on any righteousness of his own since God's righteousness is 'taking seriously man's will for communion with God and coming to meet it on his part.'"

We can appropriate this prayer whenever our relationship with God is threatened by God's apparent failure to act in our best interest. It allows the expression of strong feelings and provokes a response from God that is based on God's covenantal faithfulness and an awareness of our complete reliance on God alone. The psalm re-roots us in the original basis of our relationship with God, reminding us that we truly are God's servants, come what may.

The very act of voicing our petitions in this way will give us a fresh glimpse of how the world should be under God's rule. It reignites our hope and vision for a better future, as we shall consider further in the next chapter.

Summary: So what can I do now?

- Identify what you most want from God and that sits within his purposes.
- Express reasons why God should respond to your pleas. Create an appeal as well as stating a need.
- Pray Psalm 143, thinking of your own needs; or use it as a model for your own prayer.

CHAPTER 5

"I'M GOING TO GET THROUGH THIS!"

In this chapter . . .

- How to assert God's sovereignty.
- How to keep God's goodness in the picture.
- Why there is still hope.

God's Not Dead!

We have grieved, we have lamented, we have confessed, we have complained, we have argued, we have pleaded. Something is going to happen!

There is no way that all of that can have no effect in the heavenly realm. At least, not unless God's dead, and despite all the trouble and pain in the world, I still believe God is alive and active, however hard it may be for us to discern. Not only is God alive, but the clear revelation of God throughout the Bible is that God wants the best for the world and he will have the final word.

I think it's important that we dwell on this truth for a little while, but it's also important to say what we are not doing. We are not trying to force ourselves to feel better. We are not ignoring the reality of distress. We are not deluding ourselves about what the future may hold. Rather we are bringing to mind the truth of God's sovereignty, in the midst of our troubles, *as a deliberate act of trust in God.*

It is easy to talk about trusting God when we feel well or when nothing particular is at stake. In fact we may slip into the mistaken belief that trusting God necessarily involves feeling happy and secure. I'm not sure that it does. Rather it is precisely when we do not *feel* like it that trusting God—deliberately calling to mind God's promises and choosing to believe them—is most significant.

What truth do we need to cling onto, then, in the place of despair or brokenness or threat? In the context of persecution, the psalmist puts it like this:

> Let those who desire my vindication
> > shout for joy and be glad,
> > and say evermore,
> "Great is the LORD,
> > who delights in the welfare of his servant."
> Then my tongue shall tell of your righteousness
> > and of your praise all day long.
> > (Psalm 35:27–28)

God *delights* in the welfare of his servant. The word "welfare" is used here to translate the Hebrew word *shalom,* which is a tremendously rich expression of well-being. It has traditionally been translated as "peace," but conveys far more than that English word typically denotes. It is concerned with the whole person: your bodily health, your state of mind, your feelings, your security and provision, your family situation, your relationships with friends and neighbors, and your standing before God. It really does encompass every aspect of mind, body, and spirit. And this is what God delights in, that God's servant should have *shalom*, complete well-being.

Since God delights in the *shalom* of his servant, he can be trusted to act in order to bring about such shalom; and since God is great, he is able to do so.

God Has the Final Word

The establishment of the reign of God is a motif that runs throughout the Bible. Perhaps most famously in Christian terms, it is depicted figuratively in the book of Revelation. A cosmic battle is described in which God ultimately defeats all the powers that are opposed to God's purposes. The establishment of *shalom* is depicted as a complete renewal of the earth—"a new heaven and a new earth"—and the glorious presence of God with people. The vision of this renewal is given specifically to encourage those who are suffering and to enable them to persevere, waiting for the day when God "will wipe every tear from their eyes" (Revelation 21:1–5). *Shalom* will be a reality in the world when it is ruled by God as King.

Several of the psalms that celebrate God's kingship provide for us prayers that allow us to affirm our belief in God as king, even in the midst of suffering.

Psalms 93, 97, and 99 all begin "The LORD is king" and set out a vision of God's righteous rule. The Lord is mighty and cannot be moved (93:1–2), establishes righteousness and justice, defeating those opposed to the psalmists (97:2–3; 99:4), and is thus a cause of great rejoicing (97:8–9). These psalms offer a vision of an ideal world, of the reality of God's *shalom* on earth. When we are in trouble, these psalms can provide comfort and hope because God is sovereign and will not fail to accomplish a perfect rule over the world in the end, for the good of all who serve God.

The Lord Is King!

No matter what situation we are in, we can pray Psalm 97 as an affirmation of our trust that God is indeed sovereign, and as a reminder to ourselves that God's love and faithfulness are reasons to give thanks and be glad, even if we don't feel thankful or joyful:

> The Lord is king! Let the earth rejoice;
>> let the many coastlands be glad!
> Clouds and thick darkness are all around him;
>> righteousness and justice are the foundation
>>> of his throne.
> Fire goes before him,
>> and consumes his adversaries on every side.
> His lightnings light up the world;
>> the earth sees and trembles.
> The mountains melt like wax before the Lord,
>> before the Lord of all the earth.
>
> The heavens proclaim his righteousness;
>> and all the peoples behold his glory.
> All worshipers of images are put to shame,
>> those who make their boast in
>>> worthless idols;

all gods bow down before him.
>   Zion hears and is glad,
>   and the towns of Judah rejoice,
>   because of your judgments, O God.
>   For you, O LORD, are most high over all
>   the earth;
>   you are exalted far above all gods.
>
>   The LORD loves those who hate evil;
>   he guards the lives of his faithful;
>   he rescues them from the hand of the wicked.
>   Light dawns for the righteous,
>   and joy for the upright in heart.
>   Rejoice in the LORD, O you righteous,
>   and give thanks to his holy name! (Psalm 97)

The first section uses images taken from nature to describe the power and might of God. It renews within us a sense of awesome wonder at the incomparable majesty of God who created everything. Fire and lightning can be terrifying because of their immense power, yet these are created and controlled by God. Mountains that symbolize solidity and permanence are depicted as melting like wax before the presence of God, such is God's dominion over the created world. These verses affirm that there is nothing that God cannot do.

The next section addresses more specifically the authority of God over other gods, that is, over anyone or anything that might usurp God's place. People and powers may appear to be able to prevent God's good purposes, but this is not the full story. God *is* the most high, the supreme, which is precisely why we cry out to him and plead with him in our distress.

The final section is even more specific in describing the implications of God's sovereignty: God will act in favor of those who serve him. Therefore the psalm gradually focuses in on our particular situation. From considering God in the broadest possible terms, describing God's majesty on a cosmic scale, it progresses through God's authority over specific powers, and finally asserts that God will enact justice for specific people. This is expressed in a beautiful image: that "light dawns for the righteous, and joy for the upright in heart." As we toil through the dark night of the depths of our suffering, may the truth of God's abiding kingship be like the first ray of dawn breaking upon our senses, and renewing hope.

The Longest Week

John's little girl was ill. Less than two years old, she had contracted pneumonia and was almost completely debilitated. She had not eaten or drunk anything for two days and had to be hospitalized to avoid dehydration. John's wife was at home, nursing their newborn, and so John was staying in the hospital at his daughter's bedside.

John was shocked at the sight of his daughter so limp and lifeless. He was sure that she would respond to his company as he sat reading her stories, playing with her favorite toys, talking about anything and everything. There was no response. How could this be? How could such a lively baby lie so still for so long? Surely the treatment would enable her to recover overnight?

The next day, she was still the same. John re-doubled his efforts—after a sleepless night on a very uncomfortable camp bed next to his daughter's cot—to stir her responses. Yet she simply lay, motionless, staring vacantly. Another night came and went. The third day came, much of it spent in silence. Both John and his daughter dozed on and off through the day. John began to entertain some of the thoughts he had wanted to avoid. *What if this is it? What if she doesn't make it? How would he cope? What effect would it have on his wife?* The sinking feeling in the pit of his stomach grew.

Regular conversations with the medical staff seemed to take place in a bubble. John felt like he was on autopilot by this time, listening carefully, asking some questions and phoning home to pass on the news. He was exhausted and had lost all sense of how he felt.

On the afternoon of the fifth day, the longest week of John's life, it seemed, his daughter woke from sleep. But she did more than open her eyes. She looked around. She lifted her head a little. She even showed a little expression on her face as she saw John moving over to her. "Hello," said John. "It's . . ." And John wept. Chains of tension and fear fell from him in that moment. There was hope. She was going to be alright.

It can often be the case that the demands of coping with difficult circumstances prevent us from expressing our feelings. We are so caught in the immediate need to cope and to keep going that pain and anxiety go unacknowledged. The glimmer of hope, the first sign of there being light at the end of the tunnel, provides the space that we need to let go of some of that tension. The psalms that allow us to cry out to God and plead with God also offer us a glimpse of hope.

Praise the Lord?

Praise is the foundation of a relationship with God and the fundamental way in which people should approach him. But what is the place of praise in the context of suffering? How are we to praise God when we are preoccupied with reasons not to and we certainly don't feel like it?

One of the most striking aspects of the psalms of lament is that most of them conclude with an affirmation of confidence in God or even praise of God. So for example if you look back at Psalm 6, which we used in chapter one, you will notice an expression of confidence that God has heard the prayer and will therefore respond in a way that brings the psalmist relief from his troubles. Yet there is nothing to suggest an immediate change in the circumstances of the person who uses that psalm as a prayer. How might we make sense of that, in order to use the psalm as our own prayer with integrity?

The answer lies in Psalm 77, which most explicitly shows us how praise of God has a legitimate place in the midst of suffering. By making a comparison between the two halves of this psalm, we find that the psalm is held together by the motif of thinking, pondering, remembering. In the first half, this meditation is only vaguely defined, without clearly specified content, and causes the psalmist anguish.

I think of God, and I moan;
>   I meditate, and my spirit faints. (Psalm 77:3)

This meditation leads to a series of rhetorical questions, voicing the psalmist's sense of being forgotten by God:

"Will the Lord spurn forever,
>   and never again be favorable?
Has his steadfast love ceased forever?
>   Are his promises at an end for all time?
Has God forgotten to be gracious?
>   Has he in anger shut up his compassion?"
>   (Psalm 77:7–9)

In the second half, detailed attention is given to God's specific acts of salvation for the nation of Israel in the past, specifically alluding to the exodus when the people were rescued from slavery in Egypt and led across the Red Sea:

I will call to mind the deeds of the LORD;
>   I will remember your wonders of old. (v. 11)

You led your people like a flock
>   by the hand of Moses and Aaron. (v. 20)

So what this psalm demonstrates is a deliberate choice of the psalmist regarding where to focus his attention. He starts by meditating on the desolation of his circumstances, but then chooses to bring to mind the good and powerful acts of God that have revealed who God is. He doesn't actually praise God directly in this instance, but he comes very close. The meditation on God's specific saving acts shifts the focus of the psalmist. From thoughts that are dominated by himself and his circumstances, the psalmist moves to thinking about the people of God; from talking about God ("God" / "he"), the psalmist moves to addressing God directly ("you").

The movement is so significant that some commentators use the language of transformation. Both the suffering of the psalmist and the goodness and power of God are held side by side. The closing thought of the psalm is the one that lingers, so if we make this our own prayer, the salvation of God as revealed in history may become a genuine consolation for those of us who wrestle with doubt and God's apparent absence.

Changing Focus

What we have seen in Psalm 77 is a change of focus in the mind of the psalmist. We may well be able to recognize our need for this. It is fair to say that in many people's experience, suffering can lead to a distorted perspective on life. Pain can be so consuming as to disproportionately engulf thoughts, feelings, and attitudes. Indeed it is in the loss of hope, the forgetting of what is good, that grief can spiral into depression. In such circumstances we need somehow to retain a balanced perspective: one that both honestly embraces the reality of pain and also looks beyond that pain.

This is exactly what Psalm 77, and many other psalms, do. They offer a means of prayer that has a balanced perspective. They draw attention to the positive aspects of life and faith, without ignoring or downplaying the negative. Rather like a camera being refocused, the total view remains the same, but different depths of field come into or out of focus. So these psalm prayers, while faithfully bearing witness to the totality of relating to God, can change the focus from one aspect to another.

The psalms of lament allow us to hold in tension the reality of our lived experience, both good and bad, and not to allow the one to be swamped by the other. The memory of comfort that is past, the pain of now, and the hope of relief to come all coexist. They do not cancel each other out, but are held together to represent an authentic experience of a faithful life. Moreover, the hope of future comfort may rightly take precedence in the light of God's promises of restoration in the end.

Praise through Gritted Teeth

I think it's very important to say that this change of focus does not necessarily imply a change of mood. We might be tempted to think that lamenting requires us to feel sad and that praise requires us to feel happy, but how could such a dramatic change of mood be entertained? Pain does not disappear in the space of saying a prayer. The agonies and uncertainties described by the psalmist in Psalm 77 cannot possibly evaporate completely by recalling something good from God's acts in the past.

It seems to me reasonable to infer a relatively constant mood throughout the psalm. It is a change of focus, a deliberate turning of the thoughts to God, and believing that God has heard and had mercy, that enables the psalmist to offer the vow of praise or declaration of praise. But the immediate circumstance remains the same. When the psalmist expresses confidence in God and praises God, it is a committed act of trust to praise God *despite* the immediate suffering, *because* of recollection of God's previous deliverance and hope for future restoration.

Let's look at one more example to see this in action, and again take a psalm and use it as our own prayer, this time Psalm 13.

> How long, O LORD? Will you forget me forever?
>   How long will you hide your face from me?
> How long must I bear pain in my soul,
>   and have sorrow in my heart all day long?
> How long shall my enemy be exalted over me?
>
> Consider and answer me, O LORD my God!
>   Give light to my eyes, or I will sleep the sleep
>   of death,
> and my enemy will say, "I have prevailed";
>   my foes will rejoice because I am shaken.
>
> But I trusted in your steadfast love;
>   my heart shall rejoice in your salvation.
> I will sing to the LORD,
>   because he has dealt bountifully with me.
>   (Psalm 13)

The movement within this psalm is quite remarkable. The desperation of the psalmist is described in terms that we have come across previously, and his complaint against God is voiced in a series of haunting rhetorical questions. The language is tremendously evocative, but with very little specific detail, so it can be used by us in a wide variety of circumstances.

The plea to God for help is actually voiced as a command, so strident is the psalmist, and it is accompanied by persuasive reasons for God to act. The psalmist clearly sees his own "foes" as being opposed to God, and seeks to mobilize God to restore justice and stand against them.

Then comes the astonishing statement of trust, expressing confidence in God and a desire to sing praise to God in anticipation of the day when relief from trouble comes. But nothing has changed yet, and such praise, it seems to me, is praise offered through gritted teeth. It is a determined reaching out in faith to a God who rescues. There is no lighthearted expression of joy and thanks here, but a promise and a grimace. In the place of desperation, even the anticipation of once again thanking God for bountiful dealings is itself an expression of praise.

Going round and round, moving forward

One of the common experiences of grief or trauma is that we feel we just keep going round and round: the same thoughts, the same feelings, the same questions. Will it never end?

The prayer of Psalm 13 reflects that kind of experience with its questions of "How long?" But the psalm also shows a significant move forward with its assertion of having trusted in God's love and a desire to sing to God in thanks.

You could use this psalm as a prayer regularly over a period of time, as a kind of barometer for your experiences. There may be periods when you identify very closely with the despairing questions. At other times you might voice the petitions for help most strongly. But each time you use the prayer, the assertion of trust and a desire

> to sing is always there. At first it may seem hollow and out of place, but don't let that worry you. Keep working your way through, until the chink of light breaks in and those words can become more and more fully your own.

I am reminded of the story of a pastor who was visiting someone going through a dreadful situation. The person was so wrapped up in his troubles, he seemed completely unable to see beyond himself. The pastor longed to help this person reconnect with a sense of the goodness of God, in order to keep things in balance and give the man strength to endure what he was going through. The opportunity came when the man complained about the advice he had received from someone else.

" 'You should praise God in all circumstances,' she told me," said the man somewhat angrily. "Honestly, what have I got to praise God for?"

"So you can't praise God at the moment?" asked the pastor.

"Of course not."

"Do you want to be able to praise God?"

There was a slight pause, before the man replied, "If I'm honest, no I don't, not at the moment. I don't see why I should."

"Perhaps," went on the pastor gently, "you might want to want to praise God."

This time a much longer pause. The man's voice softened. "Well, I suppose, yes. It would be good to want to praise God."

"Very well then. That is where we begin. For today, that is your praise."

Summary: So what can I do now?

- Use Psalm 97 to proclaim God's sovereignty.
- Imagine what it will be like to have a renewed sense of God's goodness, even if you don't have it now.
- Use Psalm 13 to make a deliberate choice to express trust in God, as suggested in the box above.

CHAPTER 6

"LET'S TAKE A RAIN CHECK."

In this chapter . . .

- How to hear God's wisdom.
- How to get new perspectives.
- Why suffering creates a fresh need to hear from God.

But Hey, I've Been Doing All the Talking

We come now to a point where we stand back from the process that we have been working through, and think a little differently. Faced with testing circumstances and a range of difficult thoughts and feelings, we have explored how to express them to God, how to persuade God to help us, and how to find hope without ignoring the reality of our distress.

There is a sense in which we have been doing all the talking, and for good reason. The whole point of this book is to enable prayer through the long process of coping with grief, disillusionment, or agony. What we are seeing is that the prayers of God's people of the past, recorded for us as psalms, provide the most wonderful resource to keep us in touch with God, even when so many pressures threaten to stop us.

But relationships are two-way, and at some point it may be good to ask, "What might God say to me in this situation?" I am very hesitant as I write this, because I am all too well aware of situations where suggesting "what God might be saying" is actually a pretext on the part of the speaker to say what *they* really think. I myself have been on the receiving end of "helpful advice" in times of difficulty that was deeply hurtful, even offensive; and sadly I suspect that I may have inflicted some ill-thought opinions on others when all they really needed was some care and concern.

So this chapter simply may not be for you. I would not wish anyone to have to reflect on their problems and be open to any sense of personal challenge *before* they have had ample opportunity to lament, to cry out, to plead for mercy, and to find some sense of relief or hope. It's not for me to say whether you are at that place or not. If you feel you have the space you need to be able to reflect and listen to God, then this chapter may be helpful to you; if not, then the next chapter is just a quick finger flick away!

Words of God, Words to God

One of the curious aspects of the psalms is that they are both words to God and words from God. They are words to God in that they are a collection of prayers that people have used in ages past to express themselves to God throughout life's ups and downs. But they are also words from God in that, as part of the Bible, they have been recognized by God's people as being a key component of the revelation of who

God is and how God relates to people. Such revelation comes ultimately from God, albeit transmitted through the voices and hands of human worshipers, poets, and scribes.

Therefore, the way in which God is addressed in the psalms allows us to talk to God in the same way, with confidence that this is a legitimate means of relating to God. Similarly, where God is spoken about in the psalms, or even given a voice, we can be confident that this tells us something important about God and that this pertains to the relationship. Consequently, our use of a psalm as a prayer is doing more than facilitating our own expression to God. It is also opening up a dialogue, allowing us to hear God's voice at the same time as our own, and thereby gaining a fresh perspective on our situation.

Psalm 19 celebrates the instruction of God, using a series of images to describe its beauty and value. The structure of the psalm makes this seem natural: three sections describing the glory and wonder of creation are immediately followed by three sections extolling God's instruction. The key image in each half is one of speech. First we hear about nature:

> The heavens are telling the glory of God . . .
> There is no speech, nor are there words;
>   their voice is not heard;
> yet their voice goes out through all the earth,
>   and their words to the end of the world.
>   (Psalm 19:1, 3–4)

Even though "voiceless," creation speaks of God. In other words, we can know something about God by observing the wonderful world that God has made. It is as if God "speaks" through creation. By comparison, God also speaks through the words of Scripture:

> The law of the LORD is perfect,
>> reviving the soul (Psalm 19:7)

The law of God is God's speech. Indeed, probably what the psalmist has in mind here are the first five books of the Old Testament, traditionally regarded as written by Moses following the giving of the law at Mount Sinai. Therefore even more than the "voiceless" creation, God has clearly spoken through the law. The psalm goes on: God's commandments are more valuable than gold (v. 10) because through them the believer is taught and finds great reward (v. 11). In other words, the words of God facilitate and affirm a relationship between God and believer that is based on joyful obedience and faithful love. In the same way, the voice of instruction in the psalms, which extols righteousness and warns against wickedness, is also where the believer can hear God speak and be nourished in relationship with God.

So with the confidence that in hearing and heeding God's voice there is great reward, we will look at two particular psalms that give voice to the wisdom of God.

Can I Buy Security?

It is natural for many of us to thank God for the provision of daily necessities: food and water, clothing and housing. It is ironic, then, that wealth can pose particular threats to faith. The voice of wisdom in Psalm 49 addresses this topic directly, exposing how trusting in wealth can be foolish. Wealth may not be an issue for all of us, but it can be taken figuratively as representative of whatever it is that we look to (other than God) for security and stability. As you read this psalm, allow it to speak to the deepest desires of your heart and mind, opening these up to God's influence.

Hear this, all you peoples;
　　give ear, all inhabitants of the world,
both low and high,
　　rich and poor together.
My mouth shall speak wisdom;
　　the meditation of my heart shall be
　　　　understanding.
I will incline my ear to a proverb;
　　I will solve my riddle to the music of
　　　　the harp.

Why should I fear in times of trouble,
　　when the iniquity of my persecutors sur-
　　　　rounds me,
those who trust in their wealth
　　and boast of the abundance of their riches?
Truly, no ransom avails for one's life,
　　there is no price one can give to God for it.
For the ransom of life is costly,
　　and can never suffice,
that one should live on forever
　　and never see the grave.

When we look at the wise, they die;
    fool and dolt perish together
    and leave their wealth to others.
Their graves are their homes forever,
    their dwelling places to all generations,
    though they named lands their own.
Mortals cannot abide in their pomp;
    they are like the animals that perish.

Such is the fate of the foolhardy,
    the end of those who are pleased with
        their lot.
Like sheep they are appointed for Sheol;
    Death shall be their shepherd;
straight to the grave they descend,
    and their form shall waste away;
    Sheol shall be their home.
But God will ransom my soul from the power
    of Sheol,
    for he will receive me.

Do not be afraid when some become rich,
    when the wealth of their houses increases.
For when they die they will carry nothing away;
    their wealth will not go down after them.
Though in their lifetime they count
        themselves happy
    —for you are praised when you do well for
        yourself—
they will go to the company of their ancestors,
    who will never again see the light.
Mortals cannot abide in their pomp;
    they are like the animals that perish.
        (Psalm 49)

After an initial call to pay attention, the second section (vv. 5–9) highlights that times of trouble can lead to fear. Well, that's pretty obvious! But it immediately links this with the comparison that we may be tempted to make between us and other people. The fact is that we may become envious of other people. It may be their wealth, or their health, or their home, or their pension. There is usually something that we can see in the hands of other people that makes us think "If only I had that—everything would be better!"

The central section (vv. 10–12) then brings a healthy dose of realism to such green-eyed dreaming: we are all mortal. Rich and poor, secure and fearful, we will all reach the end of our lives. The psalmist was able to affirm that wealth is of no use to you beyond death; how much more can we affirm that, through the gift of eternal life in Christ Jesus, we have a hope that lies beyond death *that wealth cannot possibly influence*. Therefore the reality of our mortality, as well as the hope of resurrection and eternal life, points us toward a realistic appraisal of the place of wealth. It is not half as important as it seems!

The next section (vv. 13–15) continues to meditate on people's mortality, but also asserts that God can deliver people from death in a way that riches cannot. For the psalmist, this probably referred to God preventing his premature death and therefore the reason to trust in God rather than in riches; as Christians we can read this with the added aspect of hope beyond death.

The final section (vv. 16–20) expresses the consequence of this meditation in a clear instruction: "Do not be afraid when some become rich." This encapsulates the twin ideas of trusting in God rather than in riches, and of not comparing ourselves to others since we all share the same mortality. Therefore as we pray this psalm as our own prayer, we hear the voice of wisdom drawing us back to the bedrock of security. We remind ourselves, as the "peoples" to whom the prayer is addressed, that our mortality and our standing before God are of far more significance than the transience of wealth.

We are prompted by this psalm to consider what things we look to for security. It might not be wealth as such, but there might be particular situations or opportunities that we cling to and would feel bereft without. These might include particular relationships or roles, exam results or achievements. The challenge for us when we are suffering is to recognize whether our trouble is made worse by fear, which arises from seeking security and identity in anything other than God. This psalm acknowledges the difficulties that we face, and encourages and strengthens us to let go of striving after unreliable things, and to trust afresh in the God who made us, sustains us, and cares for us. The ways of God are far beyond human plans and fortunes, as our next psalm also helps us to grasp.

A Change of Heart

Pain and distress can distort our thinking about ourselves, about others, and about God. When we get into a cycle of negative thinking and frustration, it can be impossible to spot unless we are somehow jolted out of it. Psalm 73 describes such an experience for the psalmist, and the use of it as our own prayer could prompt us to have a change of heart also. As the psalm is quite long, just some key verses are reproduced here.

Truly God is good to the upright,
        to those who are pure in heart.
But as for me, my feet had almost stumbled;
        my steps had nearly slipped.
For I was envious of the arrogant;
        I saw the prosperity of the wicked.

For they have no pain;
        their bodies are sound and sleek.

All in vain I have kept my heart clean
        and washed my hands in innocence.
For all day long I have been plagued,
        and am punished every morning.

If I had said, "I will talk on in this way,"
        I would have been untrue to the circle of
                your children.
But when I thought how to understand this,
        it seemed to me a wearisome task,
until I went into the sanctuary of God;
        then I perceived their end.
Truly you set them in slippery places;
        you make them fall to ruin.
How they are destroyed in a moment,
        swept away utterly by terrors!
They are like a dream when one awakes;
        on awaking you despise their phantoms.

When my soul was embittered,
        when I was pricked in heart,

I was stupid and ignorant;
  I was like a brute beast toward you.
Nevertheless I am continually with you;
  you hold my right hand.
You guide me with your counsel,
  and afterward you will receive me
      with honor.
Whom have I in heaven but you?
  And there is nothing on earth that I desire
      other than you.
My flesh and my heart may fail,
  but God is the strength of my heart and my
      portion forever.

Indeed, those who are far from you will perish;
  you put an end to those who are false to you.
But for me it is good to be near God;
  I have made the Lord GOD my refuge,
  to tell of all your works. (Psalm 73:1–4, 13–28)

The psalm tells a story of how the psalmist was plagued by comparisons with others, not the wealthy this time but the wicked, those who flout God's ways and serve only their own ends. The opening section expresses this plainly. It is followed by a lengthy description of the wicked (in the verses I've left out), stating how everything seems to go well for them. Consequently the psalmist finds himself wondering why he has bothered being faithful to God (v. 13 above).

We ourselves might identify with this sentiment. The Christian life is not necessarily an easy one, and some of our troubles are related to our faith. When we see those who ignore God prospering in life and seeming to avoid the problems we face, we might well

wonder why we bother. Faith can be sorely tested at
such times.

A moment of revelation came for the psalmist
when he went to the "sanctuary of God" (v. 17), pre-
sumably in order to worship God. There it seems he
reconnected with a fundamental truth: that God holds
people to account. Wickedness does have its consequences and faithfulness does have its reward. Not
much detail is given here about what happened or
what the psalmist thought about, but the change in
his experience of God is powerfully retold in the following section (vv. 21–28).

He now recognizes that in his envy of the wicked,
he had been embittered, stupid, ignorant, and like a
brute beast. Now, however, he is confident in God's
goodness again and content to be with God, rejoicing
over God's care and provision. The closing sentiment,
"for me it is good to be near God," stands in contrast
to the previous situation where the psalmist felt that
it was actually better to be without God. As we have
seen before, there is a distinct change of focus, away
from the pain of the past and present, toward a future
of hope and restoration. The trouble of the present
remains, but the confidence in God's ability to bring
justice in the end gives the psalmist a more settled and
confident perspective on his present trouble. His negative appraisal of it no longer overwhelms him.

Using this psalm as our own prayer invites us to
go on a journey with the psalmist. There is no accusation here—only an opportunity to see whether we
have, quite understandably, fallen prey to the same
temptations that the psalmist did. If we have become
embittered in our suffering, or envious of those who

seem to fare better than us, it can be of great benefit to recognize this through the eyes of another. Equally, the story of the psalmist's change of heart can be a mirror for our own story. As the psalmist had a moment of clarity at the sanctuary, where might we go, or what might we do, to help us to expose any unhealthy roots in our own attitudes? Perhaps when we least feel like offering worship to God is the very time that we might benefit from it the most. Let us allow God the opportunity to soften our hearts, and receive the comfort and reassurances we need in the light of our troubles.

Having reached the point of acknowledging the role of "the wicked" in our sufferings (albeit only insofar as our attitude toward them is concerned), we must now address the really difficult question that we have been putting off. How do we pray about other people who cause our distress?

Summary: So what can I do now?

- Consider whether your distress has distorted your perspective on life.
- Let God speak to you through Psalms 49 and 73.
- Ask God for his wisdom to illuminate your context.

CHAPTER 7

"EVERY DAY IS A BATTLE."

In this chapter . . .

- How to respond to evil.
- How to deal with hatred.
- Why God's vengeance is not
  vindictive.

Welcome back to those who skipped the last chapter!

When we are suffering, we often use the language of conflict. "I'm soldiering on." "I'm not going to be beaten by this." "Life's an uphill struggle." "It seems to have got the better of me." There is an almost universal image of coping with difficulty being like a battle of some sort. And this begs the question: What or whom are we battling against? And how should we do that?

In some ways, the whole point of this book is to equip you in that struggle, particularly from a spiritual perspective. We might say that the ways of praying that we are exploring are "weapons" with which we can stand firm in the face of the assaults of . . . well, of whom or what?

In chapter three we explored the possibility that it might seem as though God is behind our troubles and found prayers of complaint to express this. In chapters two and six we asked whether anything within us was contributing to our distress and used psalms that would help us to pray about that. But if it's not God and it's not us that causes our trouble, who else is there? And how should we pray about them? There are two possible ways of identifying our "opponent," though curiously they will lead us to the same type of prayer.

Powers of Darkness

The consistent witness of the Bible is that there are forces that oppose God's good and perfect purposes in the world. They can most readily be characterized as "evil," and I am sure that most of us will have our own concept of what that is. Evil is the root of harm and destruction; it breaks up and creates discord, it destroys and causes pain, it accuses and stands over against people's well-being.

In the Old Testament God is depicted as a warrior king who fights against his enemies in order to protect and preserve his people (Psalm 97). In figurative visions, God's enemies are depicted as beasts that fight against God and his people but are ultimately defeated (Daniel 7). The figure of the satan, or "accuser," appears in the book of Job as one who is under God's authority but nevertheless causes suffering in the world.

In the New Testament, the satan has become the figure of the devil who personifies evil. The death and resurrection of Jesus is depicted as a defeat of the powers of evil (Colossians 2:15; Hebrews 2:14–15), and St. Paul therefore writes that

> our struggle is not against enemies of blood and flesh,
> but against the rulers, against the authorities, against the

cosmic powers of this present darkness, against the spiritual forces of evil in the heavenly places. (Ephesians 6:12)

The figurative language of beasts appears again in the book of the Revelation to St. John, in which again God and angels are depicted as battling and overcoming forces of evil.

In this context we may rightly see our troubles as manifestations of spiritual forces of evil, of all that is opposed to God's good purposes for the world. We may therefore pray against the power of the "enemy," by which we mean the spiritual enemy that lies behind the source of our trouble. We would want to ask God to oppose our enemy and to fight for us. In chapter four we looked at Psalm 143 as a means of expressing our requests for help to God. However, a few verses near the beginning of the psalm were omitted, including these:

> For the enemy has pursued me,
> > crushing my life to the ground,
> > making me sit in darkness like those
> > > long dead.
> Therefore my spirit faints within me;
> > my heart within me is appalled.
> > > (Psalm 143:3–4)

So what we can now see is that praying Psalm 143 is a way of dealing with "the enemy," which is identified impersonally. We may therefore use our imagination in allowing "the enemy" to represent any of a wide range of possibilities that suits our situation. Perhaps "the enemy" is some unseen spiritual force that assails us. Perhaps "the enemy" is the illness or addiction that we struggle with or the financial burden that we bear. Perhaps "the enemy" is a structure, organization, or system that seems to work against our interests. These are not necessarily all "evil" things, but they may well form the focus of our pain and struggle. We can therefore identify them as "the enemy" when we are asking God to do something about them and give us relief from our distress.

Agents of Evil

However, we must also recognize that evil is manifested in ways that affect us directly, most particularly through the actions of other people. Sometimes this is so persistent that a person may be commonly regarded as "evil." Several notorious criminals and dictators fall into this category, of course, but more often we experience harm, or feel hurt, at the hands of much more "ordinary" people, perhaps even those known to us. In these instances, we may not go so far as to label them "evil," but would nevertheless recognize that there is some evil acting through them that causes us harm.

In such cases we may not find it possible to make a distinction in our minds between the person and the evil that they do. The more serious the offense, the more this is likely to be the case. I experienced this myself recently on visiting a World War II museum in France. Even though I was already very familiar with the subject, I felt myself burning with rage and pain afresh as I read of the brutal oppression, cruel mistreatment, and eventual murder of Jews and resistance

fighters at the hands of the German army. In that moment of stomach-turning horror, the words that came
to mind were from Psalm 139, which we considered
earlier: "I hate them with perfect hatred; I count them
my enemies" (Psalm 139:22).

It is perfectly normal that when we, or those we
care for, suffer at the hands of others, we are filled with
deeply negative feelings toward the perpetrators. As
with having negative feelings toward God, it is important that we *recognize* and *express* such feelings. This
helps us to cope with them and allows us to be more
careful about whether and how we act upon them.

Once again we find that this is what the psalmists
did. Whether the ancient Israelites made any clear distinction in their own minds between spiritual forces
of evil and the actual people who opposed them, we
cannot say for sure. What they did do in prayer to God
was vividly express their pain and distress about what
other people did to them. Let's look at a particular example and think about how we might make use of it
as our own prayer.

Do you indeed decree what is right, you gods?
    Do you judge people fairly?
No, in your hearts you devise wrongs;
    your hands deal out violence on earth.

The wicked go astray from the womb;
    they err from their birth, speaking lies.
They have venom like the venom of a serpent,
    like the deaf adder that stops its ear,
so that it does not hear the voice of charmers
    or of the cunning enchanter.

O God, break the teeth in their mouths;
> tear out the fangs of the young lions,
>> O Lord!

Let them vanish like water that runs away;
> like grass let them be trodden down and
>> wither.

Let them be like the snail that dissolves
>> into slime;
> like the untimely birth that never sees
>> the sun.

Sooner than your pots can feel the heat of thorns,
> whether green or ablaze, may he sweep
>> them away!

The righteous will rejoice when they see
>> vengeance done;
> they will bathe their feet in the blood of the
>> wicked.

People will say, "Surely there is a reward for the
> righteous;
> surely there is a God who judges on earth."
>> (Psalm 58)

At first sight this prayer appears to be bloodthirsty and a cry for vengeance. It is appropriate to note that, and I would not wish to ever become too comfortable with psalms such as this. Partly this is due to our Christian understanding of judgment being different from an ancient Israelite understanding. The psalmist probably had no concept of resurrection, and therefore expected to see God's justice being worked out within mortal lifetimes. A Christian perspective would see judgment as being reserved for the day of resurrection when Christ returns, and therefore would not necessarily expect every wrong to be put right here and now. Nevertheless, we still believe that God is concerned about what happens in the world, and is still working for the good of all. Therefore this psalm is a genuine and useful prayer for those who are suffering and have no recourse to justice, other than from God alone.

The opening section of the prayer describes "the wicked" and is not shy of expressing disdain toward them. This leads to the central section (vv. 6–7) that petitions God to act against them. When we suffer at the hands of others, perhaps through bullying or vandalism, this might well express what we feel we need from God. It is very significant that the request for help is directed toward God.

Note what the psalm actually asks God to do: to break the power of the wicked, expressed figuratively as "break the teeth in their mouths." This is actually quite a reasonable thing to ask of God in the face of evil. This is not seeking to repay evil with evil, nor even to avenge, but simply to inhibit the power of those who do evil. In other psalms a similar sentiment is expressed: that God should thwart the plans of others such that they fall victim to their own mischief (see Psalms 9:15; 35:8; 141:10).

It really is remarkable that this is not the prayer of someone who wants to take matters into their own hands. We can regularly find news reports of someone who has been wronged, and who certainly does want to take matters into their own hands. Only recently I read of a relative of a victim who said that she hoped the perpetrator's time in jail would be as unpleasant as possible. Such feelings are very real and powerful, and can lead us to want to do wrong ourselves out of a desire for justice. How valuable it is, then, that we can use a prayer that hands over responsibility for justice to God, and looks to God alone to overcome evil.

So the power and significance of using this prayer when affected by the malicious actions of others is that it does not seek punishment of the wrongdoer and vengeance for its own sake. Rather it is concerned for restorative justice, through which those who deliberately abuse their power over others find either that power taken away from them, or that they themselves suffer the fate they would have inflicted on others. This is evident in the closing of the psalm, which anticipates the rejoicing that will accompany the enactment of justice.

So this psalm takes the natural response of someone suffering at the hands of others, the need for justice, and directs it toward a reliance on God to meet that need. It takes seriously the presence of evil in the world and the need to actively oppose it. After all, if God does not deal with wickedness, what reason is there to live righteously? Those who are seeking to live rightly, and are suffering because of others' wrongdoing, can use this psalm to move God to act on their behalf. Evil can ultimately be overcome by God alone and so the right response to evil is to implore God to do something about it, to change those who perpetrate evil.

A few years ago, the members of my church were very upset by several nights of rioting that had gone on in London, culminating in a night of very severe damage to our local town center. I am sure that as we gathered for worship on Sunday, we shared a range of feelings of bewilderment, insecurity, and anger. And so I led us in praying Psalm 59 together, as a way of laying those feelings before God and giving some shape to our desire that God would respond. The psalm allowed us to refer to what had happened—"Each evening they come back, howling like dogs and prowling about the city" (v. 6)—and ask God to respond—"Make them totter by your power, and bring them down, O Lord, our shield" (v. 11)—based on an assurance of God's goodness—"O my strength, I will sing praises to you, for you, O God, are my fortress, the God who shows me steadfast love" (v. 17).

But didn't Jesus teach us to love our enemies?

Yes indeed. And in fact, there are closer parallels between this idea and the psalms than you might think.

"Pray for those who persecute you."

The crux of the issue is how to pray. Jesus taught his followers to forgive others, but as we have already noted, Jesus also made an example of a persistent widow in order to comment "And will not God grant justice to his chosen ones who cry to him day and night?" Thus Jesus taught both that we should forgive and that we should cry to God for justice. He exemplified this on the cross, as he prayed for forgiveness for those who crucified him and cried out to God in the words of Psalm 22.

Forgiveness and relinquishment

To forgive someone can be depicted as a letting go: letting go of a grudge, letting go of ill will, letting go of that person's harmful influence. Within the "enemy" psalms there is also a clear letting go, a letting go of the right to exact retribution. So there is something very similar between forgiving a person and handing over to God the responsibility for enacting justice. Praying for justice (i.e. judgment on those who do wrong) does not preclude the possibility of reconciliation with enemies. However, just as forgiveness will be necessary for reconciliation, it may be that the consequences of wrongdoing also have to be accepted if reconciliation is to happen.

Does loving our enemies make it easy for them?

When Paul takes up Jesus's sentiment of loving enemies in Romans 12:19–20, he quotes Proverbs 25:21–22, suggesting that kindness shown to "enemies" will "heap burning coals on their heads." This may be taken to imply that showing kindness to a wrongdoer does not prevent them from having to face the consequences of their wrongdoing. If anything, it may worsen the consequences for them. This compares with the desire in the psalms that the wicked "fall into their own traps."

Blessing and bringing to God

In some sense, to bless a person is to put them into God's hands, with a particular desire that they may receive from God's goodness. A prayer that "enemies" may be thwarted by God has a different focus—a concern for justice—but the underlying principle is the same: to put them into God's hands. The fact is that God's concern for justice and God's desire to bless always go hand in hand. As the writer to the Hebrews comments, "It is a fearful thing to fall into the hands of the living God" (Hebrews 10:31). Therefore our love for our enemies may find expression in our forgiving them and in our praying that their fate may be "in God's hands."

"I Feel Like Killing Her!"

Sarah had been involved at church for several years and was very committed in various ways. She had recently been asked to work on a particular church project with Pauline, with whom she was vaguely acquainted but did not know well. Let's listen to Sarah's story.

> I was a bit apprehensive about working with Pauline because I didn't know her well. So I took quite a bit of trouble to be nice to her and to be cooperative. I knew she worked unusual hours, so I made sure that I fitted in with her, even though it wasn't always convenient for me. She never expressed any particularly strong opinions, but seemed happy to work with me, and we made progress with our arrangements. I made several decisions based on what we had discussed and sent her an e-mail to explain.

> I didn't hear anything from her for a week or so, but thought nothing of it. I left a couple of messages for her and got no response. I was worried she might be ill, and was relieved to see her at church, but immediately got the impression she was avoiding me. After the service she left too quickly for me to catch her. I then discovered from others that she had been complaining about me and accusing me of ignoring her opinions. I felt both embarrassed and irritated by this, but wanted to try to put things right, so I went round to call on her. Somewhat apprehensively I waited on her doorstep, only to be met with, "If you can't treat me with respect, then don't bother," and the door slammed in my face.

At that moment I was probably more angry than I have ever been in my life. I was livid. In the intensity of the moment, I would probably have said that I felt like killing her! Such an obnoxious way to behave, and a completely unreasonable way of dealing with whatever had bothered her. This was someone I had made a lot of effort for, and whom I was beginning to regard as a friend. I wasn't just hurt, I was betrayed.

I felt debilitated by my rage. I was seething with it, and I knew that it would fester if I could not deal with it. I went home and turned to the one place where I knew my feelings could find expression: the psalmist who was betrayed. Very slowly and deliberately, I prayed Psalm 55, laying openly before God the intense anger that I felt toward my Christian sister at that moment.

> It is not enemies who taunt me—
>   I could bear that;
> it is not adversaries who deal insolently
>   with me—
>   I could hide from them.
> But it is you, my equal,
>   my companion, my familiar friend,
> with whom I kept pleasant company;
>   we walked in the house of God with the
>   throng.
> Let death come upon them;
>   let them go down alive to Sheol;
>   for evil is in their homes and in their hearts.
> But I call upon God,
>   and the LORD will save me. (Psalm 55:12–16)

Being able to pray this psalm was a vital safety valve for me. It expressed and legitimated my feelings, brought them before God, and left the matter in God's hands. I would never have done Pauline any harm, but I desperately needed to lay before God the fact that I felt like doing so. The problem was no longer mine, and as my feelings subsided I was able to move on.

Mind your language!

We may well be put off using such psalms due to the strength of the language, for example in 58:7–10. How can any Christian reasonably pray for the untimely death of others? You may find it helpful to think through the following aspects:

But this is how I feel . . .

It may be that you really do feel like this at times (see Sarah's story). It would be better that such feelings find expression than be repressed; and better that they find expression in the "safe" context of a biblical prayer rather than an unbounded outpouring of pain and hatred.

Exaggeration

The strength of language necessarily matches a seriousness of situation. It represents a desperate and rhetorically formed plea for God to act, but is not necessarily prescriptive. It does not preclude the possibility of reconciliation with, and redemption for, the "wicked." As discussed above, there may be scope for distinguishing the agents of evil, for whom we desire redemption, from the spiritual forces of evil, which God has already condemned to destruction (cf. Ephesians 6:12; Colossians 2:15).

Image and Idiom

The very unfamiliarity of the language tends to lead us to a literal reading when a figurative one may well be the intention. Bathing feet in blood (58:10) may seem repulsive and abhorrent, but if we translate it into a modern idiom and say "they will dance on the graves of the wicked," it will be easier to read it as a figurative expression of a desire for restorative justice.

Praying for Others Who Suffer

Many times people have told me that they find it almost impossible to pray, not because of what they have experienced, but because of what has been done to people they love and care about. Such are their feelings of confusion and horror and rage that they scarcely know how to begin to pray. Equally it can be very difficult to pray for those who are affected by conflict or mistreatment, whether individuals known closely to us, or more broadly the people of other countries. The "enemy" psalms offer us a means to do that, by praying such psalms through the eyes of those who are suffering at the hands of evil forces. We can identify with them in their anguish and cry out to God on their behalf. Whenever the psalm says "I," we can pray it on behalf of the person to whom it applies, not thinking of ourselves but of them and of their distress. In this way we bring the needs of the people we care about before God, and ensure that the pain we feel on their behalf does not distance us from God.

Being frank and forthright in this way about those who do harm turns our attention to what God is doing in response. So we look next at how we might pray in a way that helps to affirm within us a sense of God's working in response to our prayer.

> Summary: So what can I do now?
>
> - Identify your "enemies."
> - Choose to allow God to deal with them, as an expression of "loving your enemies."
> - Use Psalm 58 as a prayer for God's justice.

CHAPTER 8

"SURELY GOD IS GOOD."

In this chapter . . .

- How to renew hope.
- How to lament as a pathway to praise.
- Why going over old ground again is normal.

The King Is Coming

In the last chapter we looked at prayers that speak of "enemies," and using those to pray that God would fight for us against those forces that contribute to our distress. Back in chapter five, we talked about turning our focus to God, and praising God even if it meant praising him through gritted teeth. It's time to bring those two ideas together, and work out how we can pray in a way that builds up and expresses a belief that God is indeed working for us.

We have looked at Psalm 97, the celebration of God as a warrior king, who is supreme over everything. It includes the line:

Fire goes before him,
    and consumes his adversaries on every side.
        (Psalm 97:3)

Here the power and majesty of God is represented as fire that not only defeats God's adversaries but even consumes them. Nothing can stand in the way of God's ultimate purposes! Such a God would be utterly terrifying, but for the fact that God's rule is based upon "righteousness and justice." Therefore as we cry out to God for help in the face of suffering, it is also right to affirm God's goodness, authority, and willingness to respond.

As we have discussed already, one of the great pitfalls of suffering is the way in which it distracts us from God's goodness. Some churches use a simple call and response that goes like this:

> "God is good!"—"All the time!"
> "All the time!"—"God is good!"

These acclamations express a fundamental truth of the Christian faith. Yet I know that it can feel very difficult to go along with it when circumstances are far from good. When prayers seem to go unanswered, when pain is prominent, when despair sets in, it is very difficult to express confidence in God's goodness.

A very well-known verse from Psalm 34 enjoins us to "Taste and see that the LORD is good; happy are those who take refuge in him" (Psalm 34:8). I find this a helpful idea because it reminds me that taking refuge in God is something active: it depends on my participation. Part of that activity is to remember and affirm that "the LORD is good." I am also encouraged by the hope that it offers, using the image of tasting: "Taste and see. . . ." I remember seeing on television an incident where a very sweet and pleasant drink had been modified to be green and glutinous so that it looked unpleasant. There was an extraordinary moment as each participant very reluctantly tasted it, and the scowl on their face gradually dissolved and gave way to delight as they experienced the fascinating flavors and soothing sweetness. In the same way, I want us to find ways to pray that help us to "taste and see" the goodness of God. I know full well that this can be really difficult, as we shall discuss shortly. Primarily, I believe it involves simply asserting God's goodness, irrespective of how we think or feel at the time.

Straight to the Point

Here's a practical suggestion for anyone who doesn't feel like praying: use the shortest prayer you can find! Psalm 117 is the shortest and goes like this:

Praise the LORD, all you nations!
    Extol him, all you peoples!
For great is his steadfast love toward us,
    and the faithfulness of the LORD endures
        forever.
Praise the LORD!

This can be a very helpful prayer in many ways. It affirms the most basic belief in God's steadfast love and faithfulness. God *will not* give up on us, no matter how it may seem. And the call to praise God is to all people. You can decide for yourself the extent to which you feel able to join in with that offering.

Even if you do not feel able to praise God yourself, you can still share in the offering of the whole church—

which is something we will look at further in the next
chapter. For now, perhaps this is a short prayer to learn
by heart, or to keep on a Post-It note where you will
see it regularly. It could be a prayer to say at certain
times of day or at specific occasions. Allow the truth
of it to seep into you slowly, so that you have a stable
rock of assurance about God to cling to as the waves
of trouble come and go.

Hear My Prayer

As well as affirming that God is good, it can be very
helpful to affirm that God hears our prayers. Indeed,
these two ideas are directly linked, as in Psalm 86:

> Gladden the soul of your servant,
>   for to you, O Lord, I lift up my soul.
> For you, O Lord, are good and forgiving,
>   abounding in steadfast love to all who call
>   on you.
> Give ear, O LORD, to my prayer;
>   listen to my cry of supplication.
> In the day of my trouble I call on you,
>   for you will answer me. (Psalm 86:4–7)

Here is the prayer of someone who is afflicted by others (see v. 14) and who therefore needs to be "glad-
dened." The assertion that God is good is immediately
followed by an expression of confidence that prayer
will be heard by God. Perhaps at times we should be
bold to exercise such confidence in our own prayers.

A common response at the end of a prayer in an Anglican church is:

> "Lord, in your mercy"—"Hear our prayer"

How might our prayers feel different if we changed that on occasion to:

> "Lord, you are merciful"—"And you hear our prayer"?

God does indeed hear our prayers, although it may not always feel like it to us. The psalms seem to offer us a realistic appraisal of the fact that God does hear and that we need assurance of God having heard. Such assurances are often found in the context of prayers about those who do harm, who are the source of suffering and injustice. Perhaps it is in the context of facing up to those who seem to "shout the loudest" and insist on their voice being heard that it is important to be assured that our voice is heard. God is attentive to the prayers of his people, and so their prayers are not without effect.

One of the clearest examples of this is in Psalm 28, where the psalm includes a considerable shift between the offering of prayer and the celebration of God having heard it.

> Do not drag me away with the wicked,
> with those who are workers of evil,
> who speak peace with their neighbors,
> while mischief is in their hearts.

Repay them according to their work,
    and according to the evil of their deeds;
repay them according to the work of their hands;
    render them their due reward.
Because they do not regard the works of
      the Lord,
    or the work of his hands,
he will break them down and build them up
      no more.

Blessed be the Lord,
    for he has heard the sound of my pleadings.
The Lord is my strength and my shield;
    in him my heart trusts;
so I am helped, and my heart exults,
    and with my song I give thanks to him.
        (Psalm 28:3–7)

This psalm brings together so many of the themes we have been looking at, and puts them into a prayer that we can make our own. The reality of the "mischief" of others is expressed, followed naturally by a prayer that God would respond to this in justice. The complete dependency on God to resolve the situation is then made clear in the statement of confidence that God has heard the prayer and therefore will respond. Such a focus on God may help us to overcome the difficulty that we feel with seeking God's judgment when Jesus taught us not to judge others. As we discussed in the previous chapter, the important point is that judgment is being put entirely into God's hands. The confidence that we will be helped by God is not influenced by any ideas about exactly what God will do.

But I Feel Like a Yo-Yo!

I'm all over the place! One day I feel quite calm and able to stand back from the things that trouble me, believing that God can help me and is responding to my prayer. But then the next day I feel terrible again; I can't see the point in praying at all, I'm angry and confused, and there doesn't seem to be any way out. I feel bad about being like that, but I can't seem to help it. Then after a couple of days, I settle again, but only until the next setback hits me. Up, down, up, down—I feel like a yo-yo! I get so frustrated that I am like that, and I don't see how I can offer praise to God with any integrity.

Maybe that is how you feel, or something like it. Well, just as we explored how important it is to express distress to God in the first place, so too can we benefit enormously from continuing to pray with authenticity when we begin to catch glimpses of the light at the end of the tunnel, yet fall back into despair when it disappears again. Psalm 42 is the prayer of someone in just such a situation, and we will consider it carefully now, with a view to making it our own prayer. (In actual fact Psalm 43 is a continuation of the same prayer, but we will focus on Psalm 42.)

> As a deer longs for flowing streams,
>   so my soul longs for you, O God.
> My soul thirsts for God,
>   for the living God.
> When shall I come and behold
>   the face of God?

My tears have been my food
    day and night,
while people say to me continually,
    "Where is your God?"

These things I remember,
    as I pour out my soul:
how I went with the throng,
    and led them in procession to the house
        of God,
with glad shouts and songs of thanksgiving,
    a multitude keeping festival.
Why are you cast down, O my soul,
    and why are you disquieted within me?
Hope in God; for I shall again praise him,
    my help and my God.

My soul is cast down within me;
    therefore I remember you
from the land of Jordan and of Hermon,
    from Mount Mizar.
Deep calls to deep
    at the thunder of your cataracts;
all your waves and your billows
    have gone over me.
By day the LORD commands his steadfast love,
    and at night his song is with me,
    a prayer to the God of my life.

I say to God, my rock,
    "Why have you forgotten me?
Why must I walk about mournfully
    because the enemy oppresses me?"
As with a deadly wound in my body,
    my adversaries taunt me,

while they say to me continually,
    "Where is your God?"

Why are you cast down, O my soul,
    and why are you disquieted within me?
Hope in God; for I shall again praise him,
    my help and my God. (Psalm 42)

Here is the prayer of someone who is wrestling deep within themselves, torn by conflicting senses of trust in God's goodness and of despair at their circumstances.

The prayer fluctuates between these two, and so represents the inner turmoil that we experience when we are trying to pray in times of trouble.

The first section (vv. 1–3) describes a sense of pain associated with God's absence. The question "Where is God?" is put into the mouths of other "people," yet it is clear that the psalmist is asking this same question too. The desire for God is described evocatively as "thirst": a basic human need that has severe physical consequences if not met. It is all the more ironic, therefore, that "tears have been my food." How tragic to be drinking only tears when thirsty for God. Perhaps this might express the desperate irony that trying to find God in our suffering sometimes leaves us feeling further from him than ever.

The next section (v. 4) deliberately brings to mind the times when God's goodness has been known and experienced in the past. In particular, it is the experience of joining others in joyful worship that has been nourishing. So this section appears to be an effort to acknowledge God's goodness, in spite of the turmoil that is within.

The tension between these two desires—the immediate pain that causes lament and the recollection of God's goodness in an attempt to praise—is expressed in the internal dialogue of the psalm's refrain (v. 5 and v. 11). It provides the means for all of us to talk to ourselves, and with honesty and integrity say, "Come on! Let's look at God. There is help. There is hope. I *will* praise God."

The second half of the psalm repeats the same pattern, instantly reverting to the assertion that "My soul is cast down" and continuing to lament. The places that are mentioned are far away from Jerusalem and so symbolize being far away from God. "Deep calls to deep" is a rich image of the innermost aspects of our personality yearning to connect with the unsearchable mystery of God's presence. Again the sense of being forgotten by God and taunted by adversaries is woven around a recollection of God's steadfast love, even though there is no evidence of it at present. This leads to the repetition of the refrain that sums up this internal shifting to and fro.

I think there's something deeply realistic about this pattern of prayer, which is what makes it so powerful for us to use. It takes two seemingly contradictory positions—"My soul is cast down" and "I shall again praise . . . my God"—and holds them together. There are no trite answers, no attempt to solve the apparent contradiction. Rather there is a beautifully and evocatively formed expression that allows authentic prayer to be offered in the midst of such turmoil. And perhaps most importantly, it keeps bringing the focus back to God, and to God's goodness, and therefore to the reason for God to be praised.

"You're All out of Focus"

When I started to make video calls to people over the internet for the first time, it took a little while to get the webcams set up correctly. At one point all I could see was a fuzzy blur, and I was saying, "You're all out of focus!" It was immensely frustrating to know that the other person was there, and yet not be able to see them clearly.

When we are in distress, it may seem as though God is there and yet is dreadfully out of focus. The circumstances, the feelings, and the people that are associated with our trouble all seem to obscure our view of God. All we can see is a fuzzy blur, and it might even seem worse than not being able to see at all. It can be a great effort to get God back into focus, and occasionally we might manage it. But like a person who needs glasses and is trying to read without them, we can't manage it for long, and the fog returns.

What the psalms, such as Psalm 42, do for us as we pray through them is bring God back into focus. They do not ignore all the other things in our view; on the contrary, all those things that get in the way of God are still in the picture. But crucially *the focus is shifted onto God.* The effect might only be slight, but it is significant. Amidst the turmoil and confusion of our feelings, so openly represented in this particular psalm, we can be enabled to move back toward God, and to allow God's goodness to become a more prominent aspect of the overall picture. It is not an easy or even a steady process. It may well be two steps forward and one step back. Like trying to focus a camera lens correctly, we may need to go backward and forward several times before we feel the picture has improved. But through the process, muddled as it seems, God is coming more clearly into focus, and an expression of praise may potentially be renewed.

Therefore, as we pray these prayers, we *are* changing. And the ways in which suffering changes us will be the subject of the next chapter.

Summary: So what can I do now?

- Focus on God's goodness, without ignoring your problems.
- Use Psalms 28 and 42 to nudge yourself toward praising God.
- Don't worry if your feelings fluctuate.

CHAPTER 9

"I AM MORE THAN MY TROUBLE."

In this chapter . . .

- How to be affirmed in who you are.
- How to connect afresh with the people of God.
- Why our distress does not define us.

Who Am I?

Going through hard times can have a terrible effect on our sense of identity. Perhaps you have had moments of wondering who you are. You don't feel certain about where you are heading, and relationships have been hard-hit. You can't do the things you used to and you've lost contact with the senses and ideas that most nourish you and make you feel alive. Perhaps the loss of loved ones, or broken relationships, have particularly impacted you, so that you feel that part of you is missing. Who are you now?

Recently I was clearing out cupboards at home and came across my old soccer kit and sports bag. Playing soccer was once a very important part of my life: it was fun, it was inspiring, it was how I socialized, it gave me targets to aim for, and it gave me a sense of achievement. A significant part of my identity was as "a person who plays soccer." But when I stopped and thought about it, I realized that it was nearly ten years since I last did so! Time had taken its toll. Changes in lifestyle, loss of fitness, and recurrent ankle injuries meant that I would not play soccer again. It was time to get rid of my old equipment. Yet the extraordinary thing was how difficult it was to do this! Even though I had not used them for nearly ten years, and even though I knew that realistically I would not use them again, it hurt terribly to get rid of them because it felt as if I was throwing part of myself away.

In some ways that's a fairly trivial example of loss. It represents the natural effects of aging, and can scarcely be compared to the unexpected and premature losses that people may suffer at any time of life. But it did remind me powerfully of how the difficulties that we face in life affect our sense of identity. The roles that we have, our ambitions and dreams, the activities that nourish us: they all contribute to our sense of self, and they can all be affected by suffering. In some extreme cases, we may even feel dehumanized by our circum-stances. Such a sentiment is expressed by the psalmist in Psalm 22:

> But I am a worm, and not human;
>> scorned by others, and despised by the
>>> people. (Psalm 22:6)

This expresses the sentiment of being so afflicted by the mistreatment of others that human dignity is almost completely lost. This can be a real effect of all kinds of suffering.

So in short, the reality is that the troubles we go through affect who we are. Nobody can be unchanged by living through difficult times. Therefore it is vital to affirm this truth: we are more than our trouble. The problems we live through do not have the last word. In previous chapters we have considered how the challenges we face can easily take too much prominence. They tend to distract from the bigger picture, engrossing us in immediate concerns and distorting our perspective on life. But there is always far more to life than our immediate troubles, and I long to find ways to pray that help us to reconnect with the bigger picture, and in particular that help us to keep a balanced sense of our identity.

There will come a time when the pain we have lived through becomes integrated as a part of who we are, but without defining us fully. We will be someone who was bereaved—but there will be much more to us than that. We will be someone who had cancer—but there will be much more to us than that. We will be someone who was betrayed or abused—but there will be much more to us than that. We will be more than our trouble.

But perhaps for the moment, it might be helpful to consider the ways in which our troubles have affected us. The questions in the box provide a means for doing that. Identifying the reality of our situation can be an important step in ensuring that our identity is allowed to go beyond it.

Knowing who I am in my troubles.

In each of the following categories, you might like to draw up two lists. First, think about how your suffering has affected you: what have you lost and what has changed? Second, think beyond that, and bring to mind those deep aspects of your identity that go beyond your suffering.

Your name

What does your name mean to you? What do you associate with it? Whom does it connect you with?

Your close relationships

Who has the strongest bonds with you? How were they formed? How will they develop in the future?

Your belonging

What groups are you a part of: ethnic, community, faith-based, work-based, social? How strongly do you feel a part of those groups? How important is your belonging to them to your sense of identity?

Your characteristics and abilities

What do you enjoy most in life—what makes you feel alive? How do other people perceive you? What are your strengths? What do you find most challenging?

Your hopes and ambitions

How much does the future affect your present? What do you wish for? What would you want to be your legacy?

Having considered our own situation, I want to offer two ways of praying that help to affirm us in our struggles and give us a strong sense of identity. They make use of the psalms both to root us within the great body of God's people and to allow us to find solidarity and encouragement in our suffering.

You Are Not Alone!

As people of faith we are members of God's people. No matter how isolated we may feel as a result of our suffering, it does not change the fact that we belong among God's people. We may belong to a local community of believers, we belong to the worldwide body of believers, and we belong to the historic community of those who have walked in God's ways. We are not alone!

We looked above at a verse from the lament of Psalm 22 that describes the dehumanizing effects of affliction. The psalm is one of those prayers that begins with lament and complaint but which turns toward praise as the focus is shifted. And so quite remarkably the psalmist, while feeling like "a worm," is able to say:

> I will tell of your name to my brothers and
> sisters;
> in the midst of the congregation I will
> praise you:
> You who fear the LORD, praise him!
> All you offspring of Jacob, glorify him;
> stand in awe of him, all you offspring of
> Israel!
> For he did not despise or abhor
> the affliction of the afflicted;
> he did not hide his face from me,
> but heard when I cried to him.
> (Psalm 22:22–24)

Here the psalmist anticipates the day when once again he will be joining many others in offering praise and thanksgiving to God. There does appear to be quite a strong contrast in this psalm: that suffering happens alone while praise is offered corporately. Perhaps that finds some resonance in your own experience.

Sometimes a separation from Christian community is enforced upon us by our suffering; at other times it may happen because of how we feel. But we should not lose sight of the fact that we are part of a community: we belong among others and they are missing something if we are not with them just as much as we might be missing out. So therefore it is good to look for ways of staying connected with others. In our sufferings, we look forward to the day when we will once again offer heartfelt praise to God among a congregation, and so we also look for ways to offer praise now. In the same way, we may look forward to one day being engaged fully in the life of a congregation, and so should also now look out for ways in which we can connect with others. Take every opportunity there is to be with others.

For now, as we seek to pray through our troubles, perhaps alone, it is good to use the expression of the psalms to keep us connected to the wider family of faith of which we are a part. Psalm 25 is the prayer of an individual who is in trouble and feels the weight of their affliction.

> To you, O LORD, I lift up my soul.
> O my God, in you I trust;
>> do not let me be put to shame;
>> do not let my enemies exult over me.
> Do not let those who wait for you be put
>> to shame;
>> let them be ashamed who are wantonly
>>> treacherous.

Make me to know your ways, O Lord;
    teach me your paths.
Lead me in your truth, and teach me,
    for you are the God of my salvation;
    for you I wait all day long.

Be mindful of your mercy, O Lord, and of your
        steadfast love,
    for they have been from of old.
Do not remember the sins of my youth or my
        transgressions;
    according to your steadfast love
        remember me,
    for your goodness' sake, O Lord!

Good and upright is the Lord;
    therefore he instructs sinners in the way.
He leads the humble in what is right,
    and teaches the humble his way.
All the paths of the Lord are steadfast love and
        faithfulness,
    for those who keep his covenant and his
        decrees.

For your name's sake, O Lord,
    pardon my guilt, for it is great.
Who are they that fear the Lord?
    He will teach them the way that they should
        choose.

They will abide in prosperity,
    and their children shall possess the land.
The friendship of the Lord is for those who
        fear him,
    and he makes his covenant known to them.

My eyes are ever toward the LORD,
    for he will pluck my feet out of the net.

Turn to me and be gracious to me,
    for I am lonely and afflicted.
Relieve the troubles of my heart,
    and bring me out of my distress.
Consider my affliction and my trouble,
    and forgive all my sins.

Consider how many are my foes,
    and with what violent hatred they hate me.
O guard my life, and deliver me;
        do not let me be put to shame, for I take
            refuge in you.
May integrity and uprightness preserve me,
    for I wait for you.

Redeem Israel, O God,
    out of all its troubles. (Psalm 25)

One aspect of this is clearly loneliness, as expressed in verse 16. However, the prayer concludes with a remarkable broadening out, as the whole of God's people, identified as "Israel," is brought into view in verse 22.

So this prayer connects the concerns of the individual with those of the whole community. By using this psalm as our own personal prayer, we will be reminded that we remain part of a much larger group of people, no matter how isolated or lonely we may feel. Indeed, our own situation is brought alongside *all* the troubles of the people of God: we are important and our suffering matters to God, but we are not alone in our suffering. As we pray the psalm we are living out the reality that the whole community is but the sum of its parts: that it is the wrestling in prayer of each individual, and the results that brings, that together make up the life of the community. As we pray our way through our own struggles we are actually helping and blessing others, even as we are being blessed by the prayers of others, though we may not realize it.

The use of "Israel" as the designation for the people of God draws us into the common spiritual heritage of all Jewish and Christian believers down the centuries. Not only are we not alone now, in that there are many other people around the world praying with us for all of God's people, but we are not alone because many have walked the same way before us. In this context, another psalm to use as a personal prayer in a number of imaginative ways is Psalm 122.

I was glad when they said to me,
 "Let us go to the house of the LORD!"
Our feet are standing
 within your gates, O Jerusalem.

Jerusalem—built as a city
 that is bound firmly together.
To it the tribes go up,
 the tribes of the LORD,
as was decreed for Israel,
 to give thanks to the name of the LORD.
For there the thrones for judgment were set up,
 the thrones of the house of David.

Pray for the peace of Jerusalem:
 "May they prosper who love you.
Peace be within your walls,
 and security within your towers."

For the sake of my relatives and friends
    I will say, "Peace be within you."
For the sake of the house of the LORD our God,
    I will seek your good. (Psalm 122)

In this psalm, the psalmist recounts with warmth and gladness the experience of being among the people of God as they went to Jerusalem to worship. In making this your own prayer, you can put yourself into this situation and imagine how it felt to be part of such a great gathering of people. Ponder the reasons for the psalmist being so glad: perhaps grateful for a safe journey, or anticipating the feast, or excited by the prospect of seeing again the splendor of the temple, or lifted up in spirit as he remembers the stories of the exodus and conquest that established the people in the land.

It is our own faith heritage that is being described in this psalm, and we can therefore make it our own. We may imaginatively think of "Jerusalem" as the church, and the "house of David" as represented by Christ, who is the head of the church. The psalm concludes with prayer for the peace of Jerusalem. Note that here we see into the psalmist's heart and those things which are most dear to him: relatives, friends, and the house of God. So we also may use the psalm to pray for those who are most important to us, and in so doing be affirmed in our place among them. We are not alone.

The use of such ancient prayers brings to mind the fact that many, many people of faith have prayed these prayers down the centuries, and we may take our place among them. As we do so, we may find solidarity and support among the community of those who have walked the path of faithful suffering.

I'm with You in This

Many of those who have gone before us have prayed the psalms and found great help and comfort in them. Here are just a few stories that allow us to identify with specific individuals who have prayed the psalms as they struggled faithfully through their circumstances.

When St. Augustine was in his final days, he was greatly troubled. He found that the words of Psalm 130, "Out of the depths I cry to you, O Lord" gave eloquent expression to his prayer, to such an extent that he wrote them on the wall in order to have them constantly before him. John Wesley was particularly moved by the same psalm when he heard it read at evensong in St. Paul's cathedral. It paved the way for his "conversion" experience later the same day as he felt his heart "strangely warmed" by God's grace working within him. In both of these examples, the words of Psalm 130 connect us with these great Christian figures of the past. They remind us that our struggles of faith are linked with those who have gone before us, who experienced similar struggles and whom God heard and met and used greatly for good.

In more modern times, Psalm 44 has been particularly associated with the Holocaust. The harrowing description of wanton destruction of life gives voice to the horror and dismay that it engenders: "You have made us like sheep for slaughter . . . You have sold your people for a trifle" (vv. 11–12). The psalm asserts strongly that the victim is not to blame for such evil, and asks searching questions of God's complicity: "All this has come upon us, yet we have not forgotten you. . . . Rouse yourself! Why do you sleep, O Lord?" (vv. 17, 23). It thus allowed God's people to pray with authenticity in the terrible events of the Holocaust, and allows us now to stand alongside them as we remember: both crying for those who suffered and knowing that many have walked a path harder than our own.

When I was leading worship on the Sunday following the extensive rioting in our nearby town center, as I mentioned in chapter seven, I led the congregation in praying Psalm 59, which includes a description of those who "plot evil." As well as providing a means to express our outrage and shock, the psalm reassured us that we stood within a tradition of God's people who have written and used such prayers.

Perhaps the best example is when Christ prayed Psalm 22 on the cross, "My God, my God, why have you forsaken me?" Here we see, as clearly as possible, God incarnate entering into the depths of human suffering and identifying with us in all that we experience. In the experience of the cross, God became one with humanity in our suffering, and the words of the psalm allow a specific point of contact for all believers with that pivotal event. By praying Psalm 22 we can offer up our own pain and distress to be carried by Christ on the cross, and there find redemption.

Just as we can identify, through the psalms, with others who have suffered before us, so also the psalms remind us that many people around the world will be identifying with us and praying for us in our distress today. We can be encouraged to know that in the psalms of lament, the worldwide church is identifying with our need and expressing our pain. No matter how bad it gets, we are not alone. We are part of the people of God, who pray with us and for us. For all the changes that our suffering may bring upon us, that much remains.

Summary: So what can I do now?

- Identify with others who have gone before you in the faith. Be glad of their examples and stories.
- Use Psalm 122 to connect you with all those who seek to worship God.
- Keep in contact with other Christians, so that all our troubles are shared.

CHAPTER 10

"LET'S GET THIS STRAIGHT."

In this chapter . . .
- How to keep going.
- How to avoid false hope.
- Why this book has no neat ending.

How Did We Get Here?

As we approach the end of this book, let's recap how we got here.

Our starting point was that in times of trouble or distress, it can be very difficult to pray. Nothing seems right and everything goes wrong. Sorrow can be an irritant that taints the everyday dealings of life, or it can be completely overwhelming. We get confused: about what's happening to us, about other people, and about God. It's good to know that in all of that, we are simply going through what everyone goes through at some point. We are normal!

Our first recourse in such circumstances is to cry out to God. In crying out, we give voice to our pain and frustration and fear. In directing this specifically to God, we cling onto whatever faith we have, however slight. We allow an ongoing relationship with God to be authentic, shot through with honest and heartfelt emotion. In doing so, we affirm that our trouble matters but that we matter more.

Because we want to stand right before God, even in the midst of our turmoil, we then lay before God our thoughts about where our problems are rooted. In some instances, a particular matter might play on our conscience; at such times we can make confession to God in full assurance of God's readiness to forgive, fully and completely. But many times, it may be far more important for us to assert "This is not my fault!" and to be relieved of any sense of shame about our trials.

We may feel that we have cause to complain to God—and discover that we can do so even in the context of a faithful relationship with him. Has God forgotten us or abandoned us? Has he turned a blind eye to what we are suffering? Has God done nothing to prevent those who cause harm? All these feelings and more can be expressed in prayer, using the words that our ancestors in the faith have given us in the psalms.

God's love for his people forms the basis of making petitions to him to come to our help. Our prayers can be made persuasive as we set out the reasons why God should be responding: because of our need, because of his faithfulness, and because justice might demand it. We ask and we keep on asking, after the example of the persistent widow in the parable. And because we are God's people, it is in God's own interests to hear us and help us.

Therefore hope may awaken within us. A vision of God's sovereignty and authority can shed a ray of light into our darkness. A world of suffering is not God's ultimate intention, nor will he allow it to persist forever. In acknowledging this, we can begin to offer praise to God, even if through gritted teeth. We can catch a glimpse of the light at the end of the tunnel, and proclaim God's goodness and worthiness, even though we may see little evidence of it at the moment.

We *might* be ready at this moment to listen to the voice of wisdom, and to take heed of the ancient advice of those who have lived through such trials before us. Pausing and listening to God's voice of wisdom is a way of acknowledging that we are in a two-way relationship with God. Just because we are suffering doesn't mean that we get to set the agenda entirely!

Then the reality of evil—and of those who perpetrate it—has to find a way into our prayers. The language of "enemies" can seem uncomfortable, but we recognize that evil is the "enemy" of God. We can be imaginative in how we understand this, so that whatever causes suffering—an illness, a debt, a longing, or a person—can be identified as an "enemy." But crucially, in asking God to deal with the enemy, we relinquish any right to take matters into our own hands. Rather we let God be the arbiter of justice, the one who alone can produce perfect peace.

Finally, we allow our prayers to connect us afresh with the people of God. We remember that the psalms have been used by so many others down the centuries, and that we join with them in bringing our troubles before God. They connect us to the wider church even today, as we pray the psalms both with our brothers and sisters, and even for our brothers and sisters who also suffer.

And through all of this, we recognize that it is not a simple, steady process. Coping with difficulties is not a step-by-step progression from the beginning to the end. Rather we get bounced around, hardly knowing how we will feel from one day to the next. We burst forth into renewed hope at the prospect of some relief, only to find that a new challenge is around the corner, making our spirits slump. We feel as though we go round and round in circles, but through it all we do move forward, and there may be a genuine and lasting change within us as we reach out to God in every season of our soul.

Where Are We Going?

The greatest asset in tough times is the ability to just keep going. Persevere, be patient, don't give up. The kind of prayer that we have been exploring is intended to facilitate exactly that. And so as we press on, we participate in the groaning and longing of all creation for an end to suffering and decay (Romans 8:18–25).

In such times of waiting and longing, one of the most difficult and painful experiences can be the "false dawn." Eager as we are to latch on to signs of hope, we sometimes prematurely assume an end to our distress. If it turns out not to be the end, then we have added to our burden of weariness and frustration. I am a keen mountain walker and know only too well the feeling of toiling long and hard to reach the apparent top of a mountain, only to discover that I am not yet there— another horizon appears further ahead. At times I felt crushed and exhausted by the experience. Over time I have come to learn not to make assumptions, but always to be ready for the longer distance. So in short, we need to keep our minds on where we are aiming— in order to nourish our hope—but also to be ready for how long it might take to get there.

Where we are aiming is the time when our suffering abates and we are able to give thanks to God for our relief. Psalm 30 is a prayer of someone who has reached that situation. But within the prayer is an account of the setbacks experienced along the way. It makes fascinating reading!

> As for me, I said in my prosperity,
>> "I shall never be moved."
> By your favor, O Lord,
>> you had established me as a strong
>>> mountain;
> you hid your face;
>> I was dismayed.
>
> To you, O Lord, I cried,
>> and to the Lord I made supplication:
> "What profit is there in my death,
>> if I go down to the Pit?
> Will the dust praise you?
>> Will it tell of your faithfulness?
> Hear, O Lord, and be gracious to me!
>> O Lord, be my helper!"
>
> You have turned my mourning into dancing;
>> you have taken off my sackcloth
>> and clothed me with joy,
> so that my soul may praise you and not be silent.
>> O Lord my God, I will give thanks to you
>>> forever. (Psalm 30:6–12)

This is another prayer that you can make your own, though different parts of it will be more meaningful at different times. You may recall times when you felt like a strong mountain (v. 7). You may perhaps still be haunted by the horrible moments when it all began to unravel and you feared the worst (vv. 7b–9). You may be in the midst of crying out to God, over and over and over again, for the help that you need (v. 10). You may be able to identify with the sense of gratitude for prayers answered, or at least to hold out the hope that one day you will come to that place (vv. 11–12).

Never lose sight of where we are heading: to give thanks to God forever. We cannot tell whether that time will begin in our lifetime or only at the final day when God renews the whole of creation. So we set ourselves for the long haul, determined to reach out to God all along the way.

So What Now?

We started out from the place of distress and from a desire, however faint, to stay connected to God. We've looked at different aspects of our suffering and sought appropriate ways to pray through them, using the psalms as our guide. I don't expect it to have been a smooth journey. Upheaval never is! But I hope that you might have a sense of being able to look back and see the road that you have travelled.

It would be nice if this book could have a neat ending—but it can't. I don't want to suggest for one moment that things can be "put right," or that we have reached "the end." I know that for some people, troubles simply go on.

However, to say that we don't reach "the end" does not mean that we are not moving. Every day is a new step in the journey and brings us fresh challenges. We have to move through them somehow, and the whole point of this book has been to encourage and help you to move through them prayerfully.

I pray that God will bring you out of the depths, but also that you will be able to grow in faith and hope as you pray your way through them.

Are we moving forward? At times it may feel that we are, but equally we may well feel that our journey is one of endlessly going round in circles, always getting back to the same place, never moving on. This is the reality of grief and trauma for many people. With that in view, I want to go full circle and finish where we started, with an exploration of Psalm 130. Rather than just the opening line, I offer a meditation on it verse by verse, which picks up the key topics of the book.

Psalm 130—Praying through Times of Trouble

Out of the depths I cry to you, O Lord.
    Lord, hear my voice!

I am hurting. I am crying out to you, Lord, because I am in distress. I don't feel like praying and I'm not sure whether I can. Things are bad for me. I'm out of my depth, in a dark place.

Let your ears be attentive
    to the voice of my supplications!

You are the only hope that I have got. I'm crying out because I believe in you. You have called me.

You have made yourself known to me through your Son, Jesus. So I'm counting on you to give me some attention now.

If you, O LORD, should mark iniquities,
> Lord, who could stand?

I'm not perfect and I'm painfully aware of it. But you know that too. You have not saved me through any merit of my own. You have shown me grace and you know that I am weak and frail. Take me as I am.

But there is forgiveness with you,
> so that you may be revered.

You are slow to anger and abounding in steadfast love and forgiveness. Take from me those particular failings that weigh on me. Blot them out completely and let me know your forgiveness. For you are a holy God.

I wait for the LORD, my soul waits,
> and in his word I hope;

I'm putting my trust in you to get me through this. You are my Lord. You have spoken through your word, and I cling to your truth. You are sovereign over the whole earth and you will overcome.

my soul waits for the Lord
> more than those who watch for the morning,
> more than those who watch for the morning.

It's wretched waiting in the dark. It goes on and on. I get exhausted at times and it's all too much for me. I'm longing for some light here. So I'm still looking toward you, O God.

O Israel, hope in the LORD!
> For with the LORD there is steadfast love,
> and with him is great power to redeem.

Our God is a God of justice who is jealous for his people. We are God's own treasured possession and he will not abandon us. We look to the power of God to prevail against all our enemies, to vanquish evil and restore us to abundant life.

It is he who will redeem Israel
> from all its iniquities.

God is our hope. God can deal with all our failings and all our enemies. God is above and beyond all that we can know or imagine. God's faithful love for us endures forever. And we will praise him, in pain and in joy, this day and every day. He is our hope. Amen.

APPENDIX

Psalms for Specific Circumstances

Almost all psalms are worded very generally and allow use in a wide range of circumstances. However, some psalms contain particular phrases or ideas that lend themselves to specific situations. The following list is therefore offered as a means of finding a prayer of lament that most readily fits with a given moment.

In general	5 (morning)
	4 (evening), 13, 130
Physical distress	6, 63
Feeling vulnerable	16
or guilty	25, 51
God is far away	22, 44
When wrongly accused,	26
or victimized,	3, 58
by a friend	55
After tragedy,	60, 80
bereavement,	88
or relationship breakdown	57
(Church) Crisis	35, 74
Money	49, 73
Mortality	90
The world	65
Old age	71
Heeding God's ways	1

ABOUT THE AUTHOR

The Rev. Dr. Simon Stocks teaches Biblical Studies at St. Augustine's College of Theology and ministers in the Anglican parish of Christ Church, Purley, England, where he currently oversees the church's discipleship program. His research into the theology and use of the psalms of lament has shaped his pastoral ministry, particularly resourcing those who are struggling in their faith. He regularly teaches church groups on a wide range of biblical and pastoral topics.